The

The Joyce We Knew

MEMOIRS OF JOYCE

Edited with an introduction by
ULICK O'CONNOR

BRANDON

Published in 2004 by
Brandon
an imprint of Mount Eagle Publications
Dingle, Co. Kerry, Ireland

This is a revised and expanded edition of the book of the same name
originally published by The Mercier Press in 1967.

2 4 6 8 10 9 7 5 3 1

Compilation and introduction copyright © Ulick O'Connor 2004

Copyright in the individual memoirs is reserved by the estates of their
authors.

ISBN 0 86322 324 9

This book is sold subject to the condition that it shall not, by way of
trade or otherwise, be lent, resold, hired out or otherwise circulated
without the publisher's prior consent in any form of binding or cover
other than that in which it is published and without a similar condition
being imposed on the subsequent purchaser.

Cover design: Anú Design
Typesetting by Red Barn Publishing, Skeagh, Skibbereen
Printed and bound in Great Britain by
Bookmarque Ltd, Croydon, Surrey

CONTENTS

Acknowledgements

The contribution by W. G. Fallon was written specially for this book.

Padraic Colum's contribution is from *Our Friend James Joyce* by Mary and Padraic Colum (London: Victor Gollancz, 1959).

Arthur Power's contribution is from an original submitted manuscript and also partly from extracts from *The Old Waterford House* (Waterford: Carthage Press, 1940).

Sean Lester's contribution is from *The Last Secretary General, Sean Lester and the League of Nations* by Douglas Gageby (Dublin: Townhouse, 1999).

A Cubist portrait by Arthur Power entitled *James of the Joyces*, which Power originally presented to the editor, is reproduced on the inside front and back covers by kind permission of Sotheby's.

INTRODUCTION

A THEME WHICH is common to these five memoirs is Joyce's obsession with his native city. In Judge Sheehy's account he records Joyce's reply when Sheehy's sister Hannah asked him why almost everything he had written was about Dublin: 'There was an English Queen who said that when she died the word "Calais" would be written on her heart. "Dublin" will be found on mine.'

Visitors when they came to Paris were always asked about the streets of Dublin and how the names of shops had changed. Joyce is almost petulant when Judge Sheehy tells him that a statue had been moved in O'Connell Street, saying, 'Why has nobody told me that before?'

Almost forty years after Joyce left Dublin, when he met the Irish diplomat Sean Lester in Geneva, he had this to say about his native city: 'I am attached to it daily and nightly like an umbilical cord.'

Even the carpet in Joyce's Paris flat was interwoven with a design tracing the course of the River Liffey, as Padraic Colum noticed when he visited in the 1920s. Arthur Power observed that he had phoenix palms growing in the room to remind him of the Phoenix Park. Sean Lester, who met Joyce in Geneva in 1940, remembers how delighted the writer was when in his daily listening to Radio Éireann he learnt he had been identified on *Question Time* by a Dublin labourer as the recent winner of a literary prize. After he heard this Joyce stood up and bowed to the radio. He summed up his fixation himself when he said that he never left Dublin, as he took it with him when he went away.

Some myths are laid to rest here. Joyce was said to have been uninterested in sport. But we learn from William Fallon, who was at Belvedere with him and later in University College, that Joyce was an 'expert swimmer'.

> He was accomplished not only at the breast stroke, but the trudge [trudgeon stroke] as well. This was due in a measure to his lean frame and lithe build, but mainly to his determination in practice . . . He asked me to propose him to my own swimming club, Pembroke [which was the best in the city]. If he had become a member he would have competed in swimming races, but he had left Dublin before I had the opportunity to propose him.

We get insights into his relationship with his parents

somewhat different from that which emerges in the biographies and in the Stephen Dedalus persona of *A Portrait of the Artist* and *Ulysses*. Judge Sheehy remembers Joyce's mother coming to the musical evenings which they held in their big Georgian house in Belvedere Place.

> I remember her as a frail, sad-faced, and gentle lady whose skill at music suggested a sensitive, artistic temperament. She was very proud and fond of Joyce, and he worshipped her. I can still see him linking her towards the piano with grave Old World courtesy.

This is a very different image from the shrinking figure of Dedalus's mother sketched in *A Portrait*.

Joyce talked a great deal about his father. He credited him with being the source of hundreds of pages in his books and scores of characters and much of the caustic wit that he endowed his characters with. Yet he never visited his father after he left Dublin for the last time in 1912. Their relationship was interwoven with difficulties. There is an account here from Padraic Colum of a meeting between father and son after a five-year gap (1904–1909), where each communicates with the other through music feelings they are unable to convey in words. Some estrangement had come between them which was resolved through the piano. They had gone up to a pub called The Yellow House in Rathfarnham, then a country village on the edge of the city.

> In the big room, empty at the time, there were two pianos. Refreshment having been ordered, the older

man sat at one. He played a theme that asked, 'Why did you go from us?' His son, 'Jim', at the other piano, played something in reply (he told me what it was, but I cannot remember). It was an epiphany of a sort, a showing forth of a relationship which was nearly always covered over, and Joyce dwelt on it later with some tenderness.

Taking it that there was that almost psychic relationship between them, it is inexplicable why, after he left Ireland in 1912, Joyce never met his father again, though the old man didn't die until December 1931.

Joyce was given to announcing somewhat dramatically that he could not return to Ireland to see his father, because of his foreboding that he would be undone there. But what was to stop him bringing his father to Bognor in Sussex when Joyce was on an extended visit there in 1923, or later to Torquay in Devon, a journey of about four hours from Dublin by sea ferry and hired car, which could have been undertaken at minimal cost? Indeed, when he was staying at Bognor he received news of a gift from Harriet Weaver of £12,000 (approximately €280,000 in today's money), and it would have been a not unfilial response for the son to have invited his father to England for a holiday on the strength of this windfall. But though he would receive in the next ten years from Miss Weaver a sum amounting in today's money to nearly half a million pounds (€556,000), there is no evidence that he used a penny of this towards making an attempt to see the parent to whom he owed so much.

No wonder he wrote to Harriet Weaver in January 1932

saying, 'It is not his death that crushed me so much but self-accusation.'

Clearly there was some deep psychological impulse at work preventing Joyce from meeting with his father. It could have been that he believed it would upset the delicate mechanism which enabled him to bring up, from his subconscious, material that would form the basis of his work. It could be a sense of guilt at leaving his father behind in charge of a large family as Joyce did.

Perhaps the emotional shock might have been too great for him if he had met his father *en face*, and seen reflected there marks of those dreadful years, when the family of ten children had led a gypsy-like existence shifting from house to house through the labyrinth of the Dublin middle class.

His wife Nora too has sometimes been represented as a sort of subservient companion to her husband, attendant on her husband's every need. She was in fact highly intelligent, spoke Italian and had a working knowledge of French and German, and, as well as being of fiercely independent character, was a passionate lover of opera and more in touch with literary matters than she has been given credit for. When after Joyce's death she met Arthur Power in Paris, and remarked as she limped to a taxi: 'This too too solid flesh,' it's hard to believe she wasn't aware she was quoting from *Hamlet*.

Dublin was a city that cherished its characters, and when he was a young man Joyce was one. Colum recalls how Joyce, with his yachting cap, grey flannels, white tennis shoes and an ash plant under his arm, was out to make an impression. He was what Dubliners liked to refer to as 'a real artist', not meaning that he was a painter or musician, but one who creates his personality for the public delight.

According to Colum, it was Joyce's friend Oliver St John Gogarty (later to figure prominently in both the *Oxford Book of English Verse* and the *Oxford Book of Modern Verse*) who helped him develop this persona.

> It was solely as a 'character' and that partly a Gogartian creation, that Joyce was known to Dubliners of that time . . . Joyce and Gogarty seemed to be engaged in some enterprise. An apostalate of irreverence! The rationalism of Catholicism and the non-rationalism of Protestantism; the nonsensicalness of Irish nationalism, the stupidity of British imperialism was satirised by them in verse and anecdote.

Gogarty, who was tone deaf, wasn't in a position to appreciate Joyce's remarkable tenor voice. But Eugene Sheehy recalls here how Joyce once took precedence over John MacCormack at a concert in the Antient Concert Rooms around 1902, and Sean Lester remembers that in their meeting in Zürich in 1940 Joyce talked of having been a rival to the young MacCormack, whom he greatly admired. (Joyce wrote to MacCormack in 1920 after hearing him sing in Paris 'Il Mio Tesoro' from *Don Giovanni*: 'No Italian tenor I know, Bonci possibly excepted, could do such a feat to say nothing of beauty of tone in which I am glad to see Roscommon can leave the peninsula a fair distance behind.')

Concert tenor, flaneur, punchinello – the young Joyce was fulfilling all that Dublin demanded from its 'characters'. But, like Yeats,* he was aware of the dangers of becoming the victim of his own image and in accepting the mask created for him by the crowd. He had seen many who had played the popular role left unable to fix their identity, to separate the phantom of memory from the reality of the future, and had observed the disintegration that followed. The artist must seek moments of crisis, when he will encounter the enormity of self and resist the mask offered to him by the mob, creating his own by cultivating the antithesis of self. Thus he confronts the buried self, fixed for an instant in time, unrelated to the past and unencumbered by the future. From this he can create his own mask, which he uses as a protection against that which the mob would impose upon him. Almost a priestly role. This would not have been foreign to Joyce for there is in his character something akin to those ascetic monastic figures of ninth-century Ireland immured in their cells inscribing sacred writ in a form now recognised as high art. He would recommend the study of the *Book of Kells* to his friends, and we learn here from Arthur Power that Joyce carried a copy of this eighth-century illuminated manuscript around with him for inspiration.

William Fallon gives a good description here of the dilemma of many of Joyce's background at the time. They had an inherent sense of insecurity often a surrogate of the colonial

---

* E. R. Dodds, the Oxford classical scholar, has written of Yeats that 'he behaved like the consecrated priest of a mystery – the mystery of words which alone are certain good. The mask had consumed the man, he had become that which he had chosen to appear as being; in Plotinus' phrase "he had carved his own image".'

condition which undermined the capacity for achievement of even the most brilliant of them. Joyce may have sensed what the fate of some of his brilliant contemporaries at University College would be: poor drunken Thomas Kettle, orator, and MP at twenty-six, dying disillusioned on the Western Front; George Clancy (Davin in *A Portrait of the Artist*) murdered by the Black and Tans when he was Lord Mayor of Limerick; Vincent Cosgrave (Lynch in *A Portrait of the Artist*) jumping off Westminster Bridge in 1909. Joyce had no intention of becoming another aspirant writer celebrated by brilliant failures in his native town, which regarded promise more kindly than fulfilment.

An episode recalled here by William Fallon can give an intriguing insight into Joyce's mindset when he wrote *Finnegans Wake*. Fallon, a friend of Joyce both at school and University College, had been a first-class rugby back for Bective Rangers, a leading Irish club, and had gone to Paris in the 1920s as an official of the Irish Rugby Football Union to see Ireland play France. His old school pal Joyce had by this time become a world famous literary figure. Fallon looked him up in Paris and to his surprise found that Joyce had been to see the rugby international.

Ten years later Fallon was again in Paris and looked up Joyce before the match this time to find that he had two tickets for the match and could reel off the names of the players and the clubs like any rugby aficionado.

Some time after Fallon told me this, he was kind enough to let me see copies of *Transition*, the avant-garde magazine edited by Eugene Jolas which Joyce had sent to him a year or so before their last meeting. Fallon told me he hadn't been able to make head nor tail of Joyce's contribution, which consisted of extracts from what would later become his last book, *Finnegans Wake*. I read through Joyce's pieces in *Transition* a few times without discovering anything in particular which would explain why Joyce should have sent what must have seemed an incomprehensible *mélange* to his friend. Then after a few attempts I began to get a clue as to why they might have been sent to Fallon. I found this sentence which now appears on page 457 of *Finnegans Wake*: 'By the horn of twenty of both of the two saint Collopys, blackmail him I will.'

I remembered that there were two brothers, Bill and Dick Collopy, who had played for Ireland against France in the 1920s. I checked in the records and found that they had both been playing the day Joyce and Fallon had seen the match in Paris. Then on page 446 there was this reference which confirmed my view: 'in that united I.R.U. stade'. I.R.U. stood for Irish Rugby Union. Stade was the *Stade Columbe* where the match was played. Then on page 451 came a reference to Fallon's own rugby club, Bective Rangers: 'And I tell you the Bective's wouldn't hold me.' In Joyce's day the Bective first fifteen contained several Old Belvederians and it turned out that Joyce used to go out to their grounds in Ballsbridge to watch the team play, which is where presumably he got the inspiration for his comparison on page 499 of the moon rolling through the clouds like a rugby ball in a scrum: 'I'd followed through my upfielded neviewscope the rugby moon cumuliously god-rolling himself westasleep amuckst the cloudscrums. . .'

What are we to make of this? In *Finnegans Wake* Joyce has loaded almost every word with more than one meaning, just like Humpty Dumpty in Lewis Carroll's *Alice in Wonderland*. 'You see it's like a portmanteau, there are two meanings packed into one word. But I always pay it extra. Impenetrability that's what I say.' It seems as if Joyce is demanding from his reader that the personal experiences of a writer, no matter how remote or irretrievable, can be valid material for a work of art. Take this, for instance, from page 115 of *Finnegans Wake*: '. . . we grisly old Sykos who have done our unsmiling bit on 'alices, when they were yung and easily freudened . . .'

This sentence has three references dependent on puns. The 'grisly old Sykos' are clearly tied up with the words 'yung and easily freudened', which are plays on the names of the two famous psychiatrists of the twentieth century. The 'alices' most likely connect with *Alice in Wonderland* and the use to which it has been suggested Lewis Carroll put his camera. How, one wonders, did Joyce expect his readers to carry such baggage around in their heads? Today, of course, it could be accessed by computer; a slight pressure of a finger on a keyboard and the information is before the reader's eye. The question, however, will still remain, how much closer the introduction of the identity of the Collopy brothers brings us towards Aquinas' definition of beauty which Stephen Dedalus quotes approvingly in *A Portrait of the Artist*: *'Pulchra enim dicunturquae visa placent.'* (We call beautiful those things which give pleasure when seen.)

University College, St Stephen's Green, Dublin, which Joyce attended, had had John Henry Newman as its president in its first incarnation as the Catholic University of Ireland; Gerald Manley Hopkins had been on the staff little more than a decade before Joyce arrived. Thomas Arnold, brother of Matthew and friend of Arthur Hugh Clough, taught English there in Joyce's time.

Newman had employed Hungerford Pollen to design the college church and encouraged craftsmen from William Morris's school to come over to design the interior work. Joyce was to remain all his life a passionate admirer of Newman's 'cloistered silver-veined prose', and never let an opportunity go by when he could praise it. As late as 1931, he would write to Harriet Weaver that 'nobody has written English prose that can be compared with that of a tiresome footling Anglican parson who afterwards became a prince of the only true church'.

At the turn of the century University College had a special position. It would be one of the centres of a movement which was transfiguring Ireland. The alchemy which makes a nation was at work. Self-government was on the way for the first time in four hundred years. A new Irishman was coming into existence, neither Anglo-Irish nor Gaelic, but a blend of both races. The welding of racial elements unleashed an elation in the national being productive of exceptional energy in those who lived at that time. What John Addington Symonds has written of the Elizabethan and Florentine man can be usefully applied to Ireland in the first decade of this century:

There is a heritage of power prepared for them at birth. The atmosphere in which they breathe is so charged with mental energy that the least stirring of their special energy brings them into contact with forces mightier than the forces of single nature.

How Joyce would have seen himself as a product of these forces is hard to say. But whether he liked it or not he was part of a literary renaissance, the end of one of those great outbursts of the imagination which began in Florence and finished in the twentieth century on the last island of Europe.

EUGENE SHEEHY

1883–1957

EUGENE SHEEHY WAS at University College with James Joyce between 1898 and 1902. He had known him at school at Belvedere, where Joyce had formed a close friendship with his brother Dick. Joyce also had an early crush on Mary Sheehy, who was the very good-looking sister of the Sheehy brothers and model for Emma Clery in *A Portrait of the Artist as a Young Man*.

Eugene was a son of David Sheehy MP, an outspoken member of the House of Commons who had been a Fenian in 1867 and had spent several years in jail before joining with Parnell in the struggle for Home Rule. The Sheehys lived in a fine Georgian house in Belvedere Place in Dublin, where musical evenings and drawing room plays took place on a regular basis, to which Joyce was invited often during his school and university days.

Eugene Sheehy was called to the Irish Bar in 1910. He volunteered for the British Army in the First World War and served as a captain with the Fourth Royal Dublin Fusiliers. After the new Irish State came into being in 1922 he became a judge on the north-eastern circuit.

I formed a friendship with him when I began to practise at the bar and looked forward very much to Sunday lunches in his charming house 'Belmont' on Palmerston Road. Knowing I was interested in Joyce, he would answer with great courtesy questions I would put to him about his former friend. One of the things we had in common besides the bar was an interest in rugby. He had been a first-class rugby player with Bective Rangers, where he had played on the wing, and we shared views about the futility of kicking the ball to touch rather than passing it to the wings, which had become a dominant feature of Irish rugby in the 1950s. He wrote an excellent book of memoirs, *May It Please the Court* (1956), from which portions of the material included here are taken.

JAMES AUGUSTINE JOYCE was his full name, but he soon dropped the middle name.

He was an intimate friend, both at school and college, of my brother Richard and myself, and he came very often to my father's house in Belvedere Place, and in the Feuilles de notre Manuscrites' displayed at the Joyce exhibition in Paris recently, there are several references to 'chez Sheehy' and to talks between Joyce and various members of my family.

As I remember him then, he was a tall slight stripling with flashing teeth – white as a hound's – pale blue eyes that some-times had an icy look, and a mobile sensitive mouth. He was fond of throwing back his head as he walked, and his mood alternated between cold, slightly haughty aloofness and sud-den boisterous merriment.

Sometimes his abrupt manner was a cloak for shyness. He refers in an early manuscript to 'the induration of the shield', meaning that each of us has to forge in self-protection a shield to interpose between oneself and the hostile world.

James Joyce came to Belvedere from Clongowes Wood College, and was in a class, one year ahead of me, for the Intermediate examinations. Joyce, the schoolboy, was aloof, icy and imperturbable. He took the same pleasure, too, in baiting his masters and the Rector that he afterwards revelled in at the expense of his university professors.

One day, when Father Henry was taking my class for Latin, Joyce was sent in by the English master, Mr. Dempsey, to report he had been late for school. The Rector delivered quite a long lecture to Joyce to which the latter listened in unre-pentant silence. When the lecture had finished, Joyce added, as if by way of afterthought and in a very bored manner: 'Mr. Dempsey told me to tell you, Sir, that I was half an hour late also yesterday.' This led to a second telling-off, almost as long as the first, and when it had run its course, Joyce took up the running again – this time almost with a yawn:

'Mr. Dempsey told me to tell you, Sir, that I have not been in time for school any day this month.'

This method of confessing one's transgressions was calculated to break the heart of any headmaster, and I fear that at Belvedere Joyce added many grey hairs to Father Henry's head.

It was Father Henry whom Joyce burlesqued in the school play at Belvedere, so vividly described in his book – *Stephen Hero*. I was seated in the gallery of the school when the play was produced, and witnessed the performance. The Reverend Rector had many mannerisms and clichés. For instance, a common practice of his was to announce: 'Any boy who cannot confidently feel that he can answer the Roman History, stand up,' and then, after sizing up with a shrewd glance the boys whose eyes did not sparkle with too bright or confident a light, he would add the dire command: 'Up Sheehy, up Lenehan!' as the case might be.

Joyce, who was cast for the part of a schoolmaster in the school play, ignored the role allotted to him and impersonated Father Henry. He carried on, often for five minutes at a time, with the pet sayings of the Rector, imitating his gestures and mannerisms. The other members of the cast collapsed with laughter on the stage – completely missing their cues and forgetting their parts – and the schoolboy audience received the performance with hysterical glee.

Father Henry, who was sitting in one of the front rows, again showed what a sportsman he was by laughing loudly at this joke against himself and Joyce received no word of reprimand for his impudence.

In the gymnasium I remember Joyce was always good for a joke. We had a new gymnastic master one year. Joyce arrived in to class doubled up like a hunchback. 'I've come in to be cured' he told the sergeant, amid laughter from the other students. 'My stomach muscles are tight from hunger' he said on another occasion when I asked him how he could do interminable pumpswings on the parallel bars. He was skilled at turning poverty into a joke.

In the year 1899 when I was sixteen years old, I passed from school to university – from one Board of Examiners to another. The Royal University of Ireland was more of an examining board than a university. A student could obtain a degree without attending any lectures.

The lectures which I had to attend were few, and afforded me ample time to browse elsewhere. The real Alma Mater at this time was the National Library in Kildare Street. We read for our examinations in the library upstairs, but there were rather prolonged adjournments to the steps outside, where we heard the views on art and life and literature of Joyce, Kettle, Skeffington, Arthur Clery, John Marcus O'Sullivan, William Dawson, Constantine Curran and many other well-read and cultured men. Meeting and conversing with such men was no mean substitute for the wisdom that emanates from the professorial chairs in other universities, and the debates in the Physics Theatre of the college in 86 St. Stephen's Green reached as high a standard during this period as they are ever likely to attain.

I remember, for instance, a great occasion on which James Joyce read a paper on 'Drama and Life' for the Literary and Historical Society. He had previously submitted the script of his address to the Rev. President of the college for his approval. The latter, finding much to disagree with in Joyce's whole-hearted praise of Ibsen's plays, passed a blue pencil through some of the passages in the address. Joyce, however, refused to read his paper if these passages were deleted. He discussed the matter with the President and to enforce his argument even lent him copies of the plays for his perusal. The result was that Joyce carried the day and read his paper without a word omitted.

A strong opposition was, however, marshalled to criticize the views expressed therein. Dr. William Magennis, Arthur Clery, W. P. Coyne, Hugh Kennedy (the late Chief Justice) and others attacked Joyce very vehemently and from every angle. Joyce rose to reply at about 10 p.m. when the bell was ringing in the landing outside to signal that it was time to wind up the proceedings. Joyce spoke without a note for about forty minutes and dealt with each of his critics in turn. It was a masterly performance and delivered to the accompaniment of rounds of applause from the back benches, which quite drowned the noise of the futile curfew on the landing outside.

After the debate had finished Seamus Clandillon expressed the views of many when he clapped Joyce vigorously on the back and exclaimed: 'Joyce, that was magnificent, but you're raving mad!'

Joyce took his degree in the Royal University and I saw a good deal of him during his time in college. He treated both his lectures and examinations as a joke, and it is to the credit of the university and its professors that, in spite of all this, he passed through successfully. He told me, from time to time, how he enjoyed himself in the examination hall. He considered that the poet Cowper was only fit to write the rhymes which are found in the interiors of Christmas crackers. When requested, therefore, to write an appreciation of *The Task*, he finished off two pages of scathing disparagement of its author with an adaptation of Hamlet's farewell to the dead Polonius: 'Peace tedious old fool!' Addison was another bête noire: referring to his summons to Steele to 'See how a Christian can die', Joyce berated him as the world's greatest hypocrite, and lapsed into Chaucerian English to state that the great 'Atticus' himself 'helpen nightly to his litter'.

It was, however, at his oral examination in English for his B.A. degree that he excelled himself. One of the learned professors put to him the question: 'How is poetic justice exemplified in the play of *King Lear*?'

Joyce replied very briefly: 'I don't know.'

The examiner, who had full knowledge of Joyce's literary ability, was not satisfied with this reply. 'Oh come, Mr. Joyce, you are not doing yourself justice. I feel sure that you have read the play.'

'Oh yes!' replied Joyce, 'but I don't understand your question. The phrase "poetic justice" is unmeaning jargon so far as I am concerned.'

Joyce and I both attended the same class for Italian. Our

lecturer was an Italian Jesuit named Father Ghezzi, who had been in India for many years and spoke English perfectly. Joyce had a wonderful aptitude for foreign languages and spoke Italian like a native, though, at that time, he had never left Dublin. My function in the class was to listen to Father Ghezzi and Joyce discuss philosophy and literature in Italian; and, for all I could understand of the dialogue, I would have been more profitably engaged in taking high dives from the springboard at the Forty-foot Hole in Sandycove.

A close companion of Joyce at the college was George Clancy, who was afterwards Mayor of Limerick, and was shot by the 'Black and Tans'. Clancy was a well-built and dark-haired son of Munster who was keen on Gaelic games and the restoration of our ancient language. He had a keen sense of humour and no guile. The simplicity and sincerity of his character appealed to Joyce, and I suspect that the character described as Davin in *A Portrait* covers his identity.

He and Joyce, at French class, made merry at the expense of Professor Cadic. Joyce would snigger whilst Clancy was translating into English a passage from a French text-book. Clancy pretended to take offence, demanded an instant apology, which was refused, and thereupon challenged Joyce to a duel in the Phoenix Park. The professor intervened to prevent bloodshed; the performance ended with handshakes all round; and the guileless Frenchman never appreciated what a farce it all was. One day Joyce entered the classroom about twenty minutes late; and, ignoring the professor's presence, went over to one of the large front windows of No. 86, threw it up, and stuck his head out. Monsieur Cadic, by a counter stroke, in order to upset Joyce's equilibrium, went to the other window, threw it up, and putting his head well out, looked at the offending pupil. 'Bonjour, M'sieu!' said the imperturbable Joyce, 'I was counting the carriages in Alderman Kernan's funeral.'

John Byrne Francis, the 'Cranly' of Joyce's *A Portrait,* was also a fellow student of mine at the College. He was a very clever man, had read most of the best literature and was a brilliant conversationalist. He was also one of the best chess players in Ireland at this period.

Joyce and he carried on long conversations in Dog Latin, to which each contributed an ingenious quota. 'Ibo crix oppidum', for instance, signified: 'I am going across town'; 'ad manum ballum jocabimus' – 'We will play handball'; and 'regnat felices atque canes' – 'it is raining cats and dogs'. And, in more correct Latin, another bright effort on the part of 'Cranly' resulted in the aphorism 'Nomina stultorum ubique scribuntur' – 'the names of fools are found on walls'. It may be that these talks were, on Joyce's part, the first intimation of the vocabulary of *Finnegans Wake.*

Joyce could have been a great actor. Even in his late teens, he was keen on dramatics and took part in family theatricals. I remember him playing in Belvedere Place the part of the English Colonel in Robertson's *Caste,* and he played it to the life.

He acted also with my sister, Margaret, in the old X.L. Café in Grafton Street in a play written by her, called *Cupid's Confidante,* in which he played the part of the villain – Geoffrey Fortescue.

In charades in our house on Sunday nights he was the star turn. His wit and gift for improvisation came into ready play. He was also a clever mimic and his impassive poker face helped his impersonations.

I remember on one occasion a burlesque of *Hamlet* performed by him and William Fallon. Joyce played the Queen Mother to Fallon's Ophelia, and the performance would rival that of Jimmy O'Dea at his best. As Ophelia, with appropriate comments, laid on the carpet some pieces of carrot and onion – the best substitutes for yew and rosemary – Hamlet's mother (who bore a striking resemblance to 'Mrs. Mulligan of the Coombe'), performed all the motions of a woman 'keening' at an Irish wake in the very ecstasy of grief.

Joyce had a beautiful tenor voice, and one of his earliest ambitions was to be a singer. His mother sometimes came to our house and played on the piano the accompaniments to his songs. I remember her as a frail, sad-faced, and gentle lady whose skill at music suggested a sensitive, artistic temperament. She was very proud and fond of Joyce, and he worshipped her. I can still see him linking her towards the piano, with a grave Old World courtesy. When she was not present, he played by ear his own accompaniments.

He had a wide range of ballads, English and Irish.

His favourite songs were 'Take a Pair of Sparkling Eyes' from *The Gondoliers*; and the 'Serenade' by Shelley beginning 'I arise from dreams of thee'.

He revelled, however, with a zest worthy of Falstaff in such rousing ballads as 'Blarney Castle', 'Bold Turpin Hero', and 'When McCarthy Took the Flure at Enniscorthy'.

Another 'flashback' to Belvedere Place reveals him, with cane, hat and eyeglass, swaggering up and down the room in the manner of Charles Coburn, as he sang with gusto 'The Man Who Broke the Bank at Monte Carlo'.

He also sang a half comic, half-plaintive Irish love song which I have heard from no other lips. I heard him sing this ballad so often that I still remember every word of it. It contained two verses as follows:

> Oh Molly, I can't say you're honest,
> Sure you've stolen the heart from my breast,
> I feel like a bird that's astonished
> When the young vagabonds steal its nest;
> So I'll throw up a stone at the window,
> And in case any glass I should break,
> It's for you all the panes that I'm taking,
> Yerra! what wouldn't I smash for your sake.
>
> They say that your Father is stingy,
> And likewise that your Mother's the same,
> So it's mighty small change that you'll bring me
> Excepting the change of your name.
> So be quick with that change dearest Molly,
> Be the same more or less, as it may,
> And my own name, my Darling, I'll give you
> The moment that you name the day.

At the end of each verse he sang the following refrain which was, to say the least of it, unusual:

> Ochone! Pillaloo! Och I'm kilt!
> May the quilt.

Lay light on your delicate form,
When the weather is hot
But my love, when 'tis not,
May it cradle you cosy and warm.
Nic nururn ni roo!
Nic Nurum ni!

Some of his humorous items he undoubtedly picked up from his father who, I understand, had in his day quite a reputation as a singer of comic songs in the concert halls of County Cork. The song commencing: 'Tis youth and folly makes young men marry', which Joyce heard his father singing in the Victoria Hotel, Cork, as described in *A Portrait*, was also a favourite of the son and I often heard him sing it. He sang these old favourite ballads of his father, too, with 'the quaint accent and phrasing' to which Joyce refers in his book. According to Joyce Senior, no one could sing an Irish ballad like Mike Lacy.

'He had little turns for it, grace notes that he used to put in that I haven't got.'

I suspect that he was too modest in this disclaimer, for his son sang these old songs with quaint phrasing and grace notes that must have been in the full Lacy tradition.

His father was a dapper little man, with military moustache, who sported an eyeglass and cane, and wore spats, and I can quite believe that on the stage he could do George Lashwood to the life.

I would say, too, that James owed his rather caustic wit to his male parent. I remember Joyce relating to me one sample.

His father, at breakfast one morning, read from the

Freeman's Journal, the obituary notice of a dear friend, Mrs. Cassidy.

Mrs. Joyce was very shocked and cried out – 'Oh! Don't tell me that Mrs. Cassidy is dead.'

'Well, I don't quite know about that,' replied her husband, 'but someone has taken the liberty of burying her.'

After his retirement from the rates office, Joyce Senior apparently devoted a good deal of his spare time to studying the pictures in *Tit Bits* and *Answers* which gave the clues to the names of railway stations – substantial prizes being offered each week to those competitors who were most successful in naming the stations depicted.

Joyce appeared to be entertained by this hobby of the old man. He told me that in the form he filled up, when seeking admission to the university, he described his father's occupation as 'going in for competitions'.

Joyce had legends for some of the Dublin statues. Of that of Bishop Plunket in Kildare Place, who has a finger thoughtfully on his brow, he said that the pose suggested: 'Now, where on earth did I put that stud?' And the statue of the poet Moore in College Green supplied with right forefinger raised the satisfied answer: 'Oh! I know.'

Of the numerous lampoons and limericks which he wrote at this time, I can recall one on Lady Gregory:

> There was an old lady named Gregory,
> Who cried: 'Come all poets in beggary'.
> But she found her imprudence,
> When hundreds of students
> Cried: 'We're in that noble category.'

I recall also Joyce and his friend, Oliver Gogarty, engaging in a Limerick competition. Gogarty would have been the complete reincarnation of an eighteenth-century 'Buck' if he hadn't been a fine poet as well. We didn't know much about his poetry at that time, but we knew him as an athlete, swimmer and author of wild verse. He was a student at Trinity College and dressed with great dash. I remember well his alert elegant bearing. He was on terms with every section of the community from the Ascendancy to the 'characters' of the back streets. Someone had challenged Joyce and Gogarty to compose Limericks on extempore subjects; they took up the challenge. The first subject was Yeats's visit to the United States on a lecture tour. The second was Dr. O'Dwyer, Bishop of Limerick, who had recently been engaged in a controversy with a Trinity Don concerning the height of the spire of the new church he was building. I can't for the life of me remember accurately which Limerick was written by whom, but I rather imagine the first one was Gogarty's:

> A theatrical tenebris Yeats,
> Went out on a tour to the States,
> He preached against pelf, but he collared himself,
> About 50 per cent of the gates.

> To him answered Dr. O'Dwyer,
> How dare you disparage our spire,
> You protestant liar, just to defy you,
> We'll build it fifty times higher.

I have already mentioned that it took a good deal to disturb Joyce's equanimity. On one occasion my brother and I were walking together in Phibsborough Road. We saw Joyce approaching us waving aloft what seemed to be a small Venetian blind. He was followed, at some paces interval, by his brother Stanislaus, who appeared to be hugely amused at James's antics. Joyce was very excited.

'Look what I have here,' he said. 'This is an Indian poem written in Sanskrit on ribbed grass, and I am going to sell it to the Professor of Languages in Trinity College.'

He opened up the book to show us the ribbed grass and the writing thereon. When he had the lattice work open in full length, a nursery maid in charge of a perambulator, whose attention at the moment was evidently not on her job, drove into him from behind with the result that he fell back into the carriage of the pram. Joyce was not the least bit perturbed. Still holding the book wide open on his lap, he half turned to the nurse and said very calmly: 'Are you going far, Miss?'

Joyce had an impish humour. He did the most whimsical things, often to his own detriment. Once, when paid to sing at a Dublin concert, he walked off the stage because he did not like the accompaniment; the fee, which he forfeited, meant a small fortune to him at the time. On another occasion, he went to London to meet William Archer, the critic, who was much impressed by Joyce's contribution to the *Fortnightly Review* on Ibsen's play *When We Dead Awaken*; Archer introduced Joyce to the editor of a literary magazine, who gave him a book of poems to review. Joyce castigated the unfortunate poet in merciless fashion. This did not please the editor.

'This will not do, Mr. Joyce,' he said.

'Sorry!' said Joyce, and proceeded to leave the room.

It was characteristic of him that he would never conde-
scend to argue any point.

'Oh! come Mr. Joyce,' pleaded the editor, 'I am only anxious to help you. Why won't you meet my wishes?'

'I thought,' replied Joyce, 'that I was to convey to your
readers what I considered to be the aesthetic value of the
book you gave me.'

'Precisely,' said the editor, 'that is what I want.'

'Well!' replied Joyce, 'I don't think it has any value what-
soever, aesthetic or otherwise, and I have tried to convey that
to your readers, and I presume that you have readers.'

This remark naturally nettled the editor, and he said – 'Oh!
well, Mr. Joyce, if that is your attitude, I can't help you. I have
only to lift the window and put my head out, and I can get a
hundred critics to review it.'

'Review what?' said Joyce, 'your head?' and this ended the
interview.

This incident is, of course, 'ex relatione' Joyce, but I believe
that it happened, as he was, in my opinion, a very truthful
man.

He also loved to challenge others to do whimsical acts.
One night I heard him wager Skeffington half a crown, that
the latter would not purchase one halfpenny worth of gooseberries in the most expensive fruit shop in O'Connell Street
and tender a golden sovereign in payment.

Skeffington took the bet and gave his miserly order to the
lady shop assistant. When he offered the sovereign in payment, the lady said in rather frigid tone:

'Could you not make it something more, sir?'

'No,' replied Skeffington, 'I can't afford it,' and he collected his gooseberries and his change.

Joyce had witnessed all this from the door of the shop and whooped with glee at the performance.

The year after John McCormack won the Gold Medal for tenor singing at the Annual Feis Ceoil in Dublin, Joyce was a candidate for the same competition. Joyce would have secured the Gold Medal if he had attempted the sight reading test, but his 'integrity' would not permit, and he was disqualified.

It is worthy of note in this connection, that a friend of mine, Mr. William Reidy, the Dublin cellist, has an old programme of a concert in the Antient Concert Rooms, in which the name of James Joyce would appear to have pride of place over that of John McCormack. The date of the concert is not mentioned. My guess is that it took place in the year 1902.

After Joyce left Dublin, I lost touch with him for some years, though he wrote to my father on the death of my brother Richard, and at another time sent me an Italian newspaper in which he had written an article – *Il Fenianismo* – on the death of John O'Leary, the great Fenian leader, who, by the way, presided at one of the debates in the Literary and Historical Debating Society when I was in the college.

One night in the year 1909 during a production by the Abbey Theatre of Shaw's *Blanco Posnet* I met Joyce again. He tapped me on the shoulder from behind with his walking stick, and then greeted me nonchalantly, as if we had met the previous day. He told me that he had come to Dublin to do the critique of the play – which had been censored in Great

Britain – for an Italian newspaper, *Il Piccolo Sera*. He also said that I would hear interesting news of him within the next few weeks. This had reference, I understand, to the fact that he was to be the manager of the first cinema in Dublin, the 'Volta' in Mary Street. I believe he did obtain the position, but, if so, he held it only for a very short period.

Joyce was very sparing in his praise of other writers; and I was surprised, therefore, when, on this occasion, he told me that he admired the works of George Meredith, and that he regarded *The Tragic Comedians* as a novel of outstanding merit.

Except for Ibsen and Dante, the only other author whom he favoured was James Clarence Mangan; and I remember the intense pleasure with which all those assembled one night in my father's house heard him recite 'The Nameless One' by the hapless Irish poet.

The next and last time I met Joyce was in his flat in Paris in the year 1928, when he had become world famous. I found out his address in the Rue de Grenelle from Miss Sylvia Beach who, I understand, financed the publication of the first edition of *Ulysses* and whose book shop in Paris had on display on its shelves many photographs of Joyce.

She was charmed when I told her that I was an old school companion of his, and she produced a photograph of a group of students and professors taken at University College. The photo had been taken by my friend, Con Curran, and the group included Joyce, and she was so pleased that I was able to name all the others, that she presented me with a free copy of *Transition*, in which Joyce's *A Work in Progress* was then being published. I regret to say that I never read the instalment in *Transition* as the first paragraph thereof convinced me that my untutored mind was not adequate to understand and appreciate Joyce's new 'vocabulary', as he himself termed it.

Later that day my wife and I called on Joyce at his flat, and met there also his wife, son and daughter. Everything in Joyce's rooms spelt 'Dublin'. There were pictures and sketches of old Dublin on the walls, and even the design of the large rug, with which the floor was carpeted, portrayed the corkscrew course of the River Liffey.

He was delighted to meet me again, and his queries were all concerning the Dublin that he knew and loved.

'Where were now Tom and Dick and Harry?' naming former companions that I had well-nigh forgotten, and he became quite impatient that I could not call to mind at once one Jack O'Reilly, who had faded from the Dublin scene for many years.

'And how does Sallynoggin look now?' and 'the shops along the chief streets?'

And then he questioned me about some of Dublin's well-known characters. For instance: 'Did J. B. Hall' – a reporter for the *Freeman's Journal* – 'still go round in all weathers with his overcoat slung over one shoulder?'

He was thrilled to know that the statue of Smith O'Brien had been moved from O'Connell Bridge, and was now lined up with the other statues in O'Connell Street.

'Why has nobody told me that before?' he said rather petulantly.

My sister, Mrs. Sheehy Skeffington, told me that at a later

date she had another such interview with Joyce. Half-dazed with his cascade of queries, she at length said to him:

'Mr. Joyce, you pretend to be a cosmopolitan, but how is it that all your thoughts are about Dublin, and almost everything that you have written deals with it and its inhabitants?'

'Mrs. Skeffington!' he replied, with a rather whimsical smile, 'there was an English queen who said that when she died the world "Calais" would be written on her heart. "Dublin" will be found on mine.'

WILLIAM G. FALLON

1881–1958

L IKE EUGENE SHEEHY, William Fallon was at Belvedere College and University College with James Joyce. I knew him when I practised as a barrister in the Dublin Law Library where we would talk about his school friend 'Jice' (this is how he pronounced Joyce's name). Fallon appears under his own name in *A Portrait of the Artist as a Young Man*: 'A boy named Fallon in Belvedere had often asked him with a silly laugh why they moved so often.'

He had known Joyce from an early age and was part of a group of young Belvederians whom Joyce went round with. Fallon had been very good-looking as a young man and, as I was told, much sought after by female students at the university. But an air of unfulfillment, almost of tragedy, hung over him when I knew him in the Law Library. He had been one of the bright young men of John Redmond's Irish Party in the early 1900s, and could have had expectations of a Cabinet role if Home Rule had come, as it had seemed certain in the years before the First World War that it would. Somewhat plaintively he would remind me that the Welsh Disestablishment Bill was on the statute book in 1914. After the war the Welsh Bill had been enacted and he believed that the same would have happened with the Home Rule Bill if the 1916 Rising had not happened.

He wore a bow tie, retained his good looks in a slightly ruined face and remained unmarried. He became president of the Irish Rugby Football Union in 1949.

WHAT DOES ONE know of Victorian Dublin who only our sprawling modern capital knows? Upwards of seventy years ago Dublin was the decaying metropolis of a neglected Crown colony with an Ascendancy in control of the public services and major business establishments. Waste and decline had long before set in commercially and socially in the wake of a Statute (1801), the effect of which was to unite the two Legislative Assemblies of Great Britain and Ireland. Thereafter and throughout the century the opulent families abandoned their town houses and withdrew to England if not to their landed estates in the Irish provinces. Save that the homes overlooking or adjacent to Dublin's squares held on somehow, it was inevitable that the spacious buildings, flanked as they were by unique avenues of Georgian domestic architecture, would in time degenerate into dilapidated tenements. So it came to pass, and the City's Corporation despaired of finding a solution for the problem. This was James Joyce's Dublin. To fill the vacuum left by the streaming exodus of the Ascendancy and its entourage, numerous families of the upper middle classes, availing of the tempo, awakened to the possibilities of improving their modest commercial activities or furtively edged their way into the professions. Daniel O'Connell's Catholic Relief Act and his Municipal Reform Association had, however, inadvertently provided those families with an additional incentive; that of social advancement; they duly proceeded to rectify their social deficiencies by means of suitable introductions to the Viceroy. The successful entrees were thereafter labelled 'Castle Catholics'. Contra, the generality of Dubliners, the bourgeoisie, bereft of outlets, were immobilised, anonymous, but passed muster as genteel. To Joyce, they were 'the obtuse middle class' and reconciled to their lot as if waiting until time shall be no more. Below was the unorganised welter of wage-earners in their crumbling dwellings. At times a veneer of colour relieved the depressing panorama, whenever, at routine parades, uniformed recruiting officers for the Royal Dublin Fusiliers canvassed the streets, or handwaves of greeting, coupled with amusement, were extended to seasonal trippers from the Isle of Man who, nervously clutching the handrails of jaunting cars, were en route for Guinness's Brewery, the site of the assassination in the Phoenix Park of Burke and Cavendish in 1882, and therefrom to the National Museum. But the mean streets multiplied with the decades and slumdom had long prior been reckoned in terms of acres. We of the eldest generation retain memories of it all. So, too, in his day, did Joyce. To him it was 'the centre of paralysis'.

James Joyce was born in a southern suburb of Dublin and was sent to boarding school at Clongowes Wood College at the age of six where he remained until 1891. Clongowes was a Jesuit institution. After an interval he arrived at Belvedere College in Dublin. This was a day-school also run by the Jesuits. He was then eleven years old. I had commenced there some time ahead of him. We youngest pupils used to be shepherded from the classrooms of the grownups and classified in groups according to age. Among other newcomers was an English-speaking Italian boy of about Joyce's own age. Both were allotted to our own particular group, although we were entering on our second year at the college. Joyce, as one might have expected, did not join in the preliminary boyish din;

instead, he exchanged whispers with the Italian boy, whom he had previously met somewhere. Was this the beginning of his interest in Italy which he cultivated so assiduously in later years? He was also to remember later with affection the Jesuit scholastic who had charge of us that day, Mr. McArdle, S.J.

After a period at Belvedere, Joyce graduated to the Upper House. He won an Exhibition (scholarship) in junior and middle grade. He would perhaps have done even better in the examinations had it not been for his wide reading outside the prescribed course. One of our class-mates, Albrecht Connolly, used to tell us that Joyce could be seen every Saturday scouring the bookstalls for new works. Stannie (Jim's brother) used to say that Jim was always ahead of his homework, so much so that it left him time for all sorts of extra-curricular reading, including opera scores.

Our English teacher was Mr. George Dempsey. Joyce always maintained that he owed Mr. Dempsey a debt for the way he had been taught English. Mr. Dempsey was the reader for a Dublin publisher and occasionally for a Catholic firm in London. The subjects he prescribed usually provided scope for any of us with imagination. Joyce availed of his liberality. On one occasion we had Lamb's Shakespearean Tales, an elementary text-book. Joyce instead handed in a composition on the essays of Elia. I remember, too, that after we had made some progress in Pope's *Essay on Man* in class, our task was to comment on the lines:

> Honour and shame from no condition rise;
> Act well your part, there all the honour lies.

'And Joyce,' Mr. Dempsey added, 'you may write whatever you like.' Yes; Joyce elected to write on Pope's translation of the *Odyssey*. Absit omen! He was no more than sixteen years old at the time. Connolly suggested that he must have picked it up at one of the second-hand bookstalls. This was his first introduction perhaps to the famous tale of which he was later to give his own twentieth-century rendering. Another time Mr. Dempsey doubtless had a good and sufficient reason for turning to Joyce with 'I am keeping yours,' when Jim, instead of an essay on a Shakespearean play prescribed by the Intermediate Education Board – submitted 'Ibsen, Dramatist'. Joyce told me that it was through Mr. Dempsey he had made contact with the distinguished editor of *Fortnightly Review*, W. T. Stead, and subsequently contributed to that review his well-known article on Ibsen's play, *When We Dead Awaken*.

Father William Henry, S.J., was Rector during those years. He was the last of the stern Victorian age at Belvedere. Early on he had systematically sought to probe into Joyce's puzzling equanimity with 'Proud boy, Joyce?' The reaction invariably was a respectful but granitic – 'No, Sir.' But no sooner had the victim been promoted to the middle grade than an unexpected relationship developed. The Rector was our principal teacher and in class Joyce, to his surprise, was all but word-perfect whether the subject was Fander's Catechism of Christian Doctrine, the Classics, or the History of Greece and Rome. What then? Mr. Dempsey went periodically to Father Henry's office at the luncheon interval. Now Joyce was added to the Rector's table. What transpired there was not for us to hear; Joyce's lips were sealed. But a boy called Cassidy discovered what was afoot. He went one day on an errand to the Rector's room during lunch. He came back with the news: 'Joyce is getting a free lunch.' It seems that the Rector, knowing of the straitened circumstances of the Joyce family, and appreciating the talent of the young scholar, had seen to it, in the most tactful way possible, that he was properly fed. There were three disconnected sequels to this event. Joyce became head of the Senior Sodality, he joined the recently established gymnastic class in the college theatre, and Mr. Dempsey gave increasing attention to his weekly essays. As Prefect of the school Sodality, Joyce with the others would go to Confession and Holy Communion each month in the school chapel. This continued throughout the years he was at Belvedere. One has a clear recollection of this, because Joyce, being the Prefect, used to be the first to get up and lead the others out of chapel on Sodality mornings.

Joyce's antics in the gymnastic class could be most amusing. Light, slim and flexible as he was, he lacked the co-ordination for games, but he enjoyed the fun and companionship of other boys; that is what counted for him. I remember well his antics on the horizontal bar. There would be a call for help from the other side of the gymnasium. We would look over and see Jim's lanky figure entangled, that is the only word I can use, on the horizontal bar. His legs were where his feet should be and vice versa. Jim's call would be a sort of a screech, a brief but penetrating cackle of laughter. When we would disentangle him and get him down he would relapse into sudden silence and become desperately solemn. This sudden change from laughter to solemnity was a particular characteristic of his. He came to football matches with us in the

Phoenix Park. Fr. Thomkin, our Prefect of Studies, used to bring us out there. Joyce would give up playing after a while and slide off to the touch line, but he never went away. He always stayed on to watch. He wasn't able to kick the ball properly, for some reason. He would kick it with his heel like a girl. When we set out for home, there Joyce would be in the van, but striding out alone.

He was a good walker. I would always go by tram to the Bull Wall to swim, Joyce would walk there and back (about 4 miles). It may surprise many to know that he was an expert swimmer. He was accomplished not only at the breast stroke, but the trudge as well. This was due in a measure to his lean frame and lithe build, but mainly to his determination in practice. At the Bull Wall where free bathing facilities were provided, he had become friendly with a fellow swimmer, Dr. Vincent O'Brien. Vincent O'Brien was John McCormack's singing teacher, and was the first, I believe, to make Joyce's fine singing voice known to the public. Joyce admired Vincent's swimming ability. O'Brien used to swim out from the Bull Wall towards the Liffey, a risky swim for anyone but a strong swimmer. Joyce confided to me that he hoped some time to emulate his hero and brave the Liffey currents. He would often strike amusing poses when he was in swimming togs. I remember one day out at the Bull Wall when the sky was leaden and the sea extremely rough. When I arrived at our bathing place, Joyce was sitting on a rock shivering. He was just out of the water and had not even dried his hair. 'What on earth do you represent now?' I asked. 'Hunger,' he replied, without a smile. Was this the 'induration of the shield'?

I remember on another occasion he came to his first swimming lesson in Tara Street Baths. He had borrowed a clumsy safety outfit from a Ringsend seaman. But, on entering the shallow water, his head and shoulders went under, and his feet rose above the surface as a result of misadjusting the contraption. As soon as he regained the perpendicular, a sudden gale of laughter, a prolonged cackle, greeted his onlookers, followed immediately by silence and a fixed gaze as if looking through us to a distant object beyond.

Joyce asked me to propose him for my own swimming club, Pembroke. If he had become a member, he would have competed in swimming races, but he had left Dublin before I had an opportunity to propose him.

Albrecht Connolly, Joyce and I used to find ourselves frequently in each other's company when we were at Belvedere. Connolly lived very near the college, and Joyce and I were within a short distance of it as well. I remember one occasion when we were all small boys, in the region of thirteen years or so, Connolly, Joyce and I were walking home. Connolly asked Joyce to admit that Shakespeare was the greatest poet. Joyce would not do so. Connolly then twisted Joyce's arm, and continued to frog-march Joyce along beside him for quite a long period. As we were going in a different direction from Joyce's home, he knew that he would be late for tea. (Albie had a tendency to be a bully.) I have no idea whether Joyce thought that Shakespeare was the greatest English writer, or whether he had another choice of his own, but it was quite clear, one way or another, that he was not going to have criticism forced on him. He was in tears at Connolly's action, but he refused to yield.

And he hadn't given in when Connolly released him after they had reached Connolly's home and he had to go in.

Companions of this period sometimes went into Joyce's books under another name. Joyce used to play Red Indians with a family called Wilkins. These became Dillon when he used his recollection of the family as background in his story 'Encounter' in *Dubliners*.

'Araby' is one of the most poignant stories in *Dubliners*. It tells of a young boy going to a bazaar to buy a present for a favoured girl. But his uncle waits so long to give him the money that the boy arrives too late at the bazaar to buy the present he had marked out for his girlfriend. Strangely enough, I remember meeting Joyce on the very evening that he went to this bazaar. It *was* called Araby. I had just got off the train at Lansdowne Road when I spied him. The train used to draw in on the main line and then go into a siding to let off visitors to the bazaar. It was a Saturday night. When we reached the bazaar it was just clearing up. It was very late. I lost Joyce in the crowd, but I could see he was disheartened over something. I recall, too, that Joyce had had some difficulty for a week or so previously in extracting the money for the bazaar from his parent.

I believe that Joyce was a little too distant to be a close friend. When he was with us he sometimes appeared to be peering into the future. But he always entered into the spirit of things. One of the most notable things about him at school was his flair for observation linked to an uncanny memory. Incidents, not even of passing interest – a house that seemed to be unrelated to its fellows alongside, boys playing at marbles at the kerbstone of a roadway, a clump of dwarf trees, a distant view of a chimney stack of a brewery suddenly swinging into sight at a particular bend in an avenue – were all imprinted on his mind with photographic accuracy.

I think it appropriate to mention here a few observations of what I knew of Joyce's religious attitude as a schoolboy and a student. Stanislaus Joyce has recorded in his *Dublin Diary* of August 1904 that 'Jim had ceased to believe in Catholicism for many years'. This to my mind is an unjustifiable conclusion. It shows an inability to distinguish between commonplace irreverence or negligence and dogmatic disbelief.

I remember very well at University College that Jim continued to attend to his religious duties. He was a member of the College Sodality. This included going to Confession and Communion. He was also a member of St. Thomas Aquinas Academy. His sister, Sister Gertrude, who had become a nun in New Zealand, corresponded with me until her death in March 1964. She had exchanged letters with her brother, Jim, until his death in 1941. She prayed constantly for him during his lifetime and after his death.

I often think that Joyce would have been attracted to Teilhard de Chardin's interpretation of Catholicism, Joyce with his H.C.E. (Here Comes Everybody) who revolves in four cycles of human evolution. Perhaps Joyce got only halfway there. Teilhard's notion that man is progressing, that science and astronomy all converge on the infinite, would, I believe, have greatly appealed to that side of Joyce's character which I feel was spiritual.

It must have been a refreshing experience for Joyce when he

joined the old University College at St. Stephen's Green at that
time under the Deanship of Fr. William Delaney, S.J. Although
joining, he had no set purpose in seeking a university degree.
Seemingly, Dublin University with its single college and
classical façade could equally well have provided for his way-
ward requirements. But no! and not precisely because it happened to be a Protestant institution, but because of what to
him was 'the otherness' of the place. He was the complete
Dubliner. In Trinity he would have been a misfit. It is more
likely, however, that his peevish comment, as he found Trinity
at the turn of the century, was that the only affluent college in
the land had failed to live up to its former reputation in the
sphere of letters and the fine arts. No doubt disciples of Anti-
sthenes could always silence criticism by pointing to 'Trinity's'
achievements on the cricket field and as the appointed
Guardian Angel of the Book of Kells! It could have been that
way with Joyce whenever he glanced at the statues of Goldsmith and Burke on his way to No. 86 St. Stephen's Green. At
University College, at least, he would realise how native tra-
ditions and culture, held in common, were the bonds that
linked his Dublin with the provinces. That revelation was
Joyce's simple conception of Irish nationalism, but in the
awakening political enthusiasm of those years he was wholly
disinterested!* He graduated in 1902 at twenty years of age,
modern languages being his forte. His attendance at lectures
had been irregular, probably because, unlike a majority of the

---

* But Joyce later took a keen interest in Arthur Griffith's Sinn Féin and
  thought it the only political group likely to succeed – Editor's note.

student body who had programmed their futures, Joyce had no plans, although he toyed for a while with the College's Cecilia St. Medical School. Later on, still perplexed by his own indecision and hesitancy, Joyce availed of opportunities to meet Professor William Magennis and during the succeeding years they frequently conversed in the precincts of the college or following a meeting of the Literary and Historical Society. The professor was 'student-minded' and used to encourage newcomers to join the Society and graduates to continue their membership. He lectured in the faculty of Mental Science and, as I knew, advised Joyce to read Cardinal Newman's autobiographic *Apologia Pro Vita Sua*. Actually, Joyce had passed unnoticed at the college until he began to take an active part in the Literary and Historical Society's debates. In those years, say 1899–1906, the 55-year-old society overflowed with a membership of all the talents, its golden age, such as, according to seniority – Kent, Kennedy, MacGarry, Sheehy Skeffington (Joyce's 'McCann'), A. Clery, Patrick Pearse (of 1916 fame), Kettle, Walsh, O'Sullivan, Hackett, Curran, Kinahan ('Moynihan' in *Portrait*), the brothers R. and E. Sheehy, G. Clancy ('Davin'), Rory O'Connor (of 'the Civil War'), to name a few without derogation of others, many of whom in the after years became notable personalities in their respective spheres of activity. Joyce would supplement any such list following his Ibsenesque address on 'Drama and Life'. Another outstanding contribution was his 'Clarence Mangan', with its individualistic analysis of that half forgotten Irish poet. Yet the most attractive in the galaxy was not Joyce but Kettle, who crossed swords with Joyce in a well-remembered controversy on the ultra Celticism of Yeats's play *The Countess Cathleen*. It provoked Joyce's pamphlet *The Day of the Rabblement*, which he published in conjunction with Frank Sheehy Skeffington.

Commentators have afforded only minimal space to the influence J. F. Byrne ('Cranly' in *A Portrait*) imperceptibly exerted on Joyce's development. They had been together at Belvedere College and during their brief spells at the Medical School. (To us he was 'Jeffbyrne'.) Yet they were opposites, physically and intellectually; for as well as being a keen athlete, Byrne's reading hours apparently ranged in compartments over the circle of human knowledge, the perfect encyclopedist in miniature. Parading the four sides of St. Stephen's Green, or Mountjoy Square, at times long after nightfall, I, on more than one occasion, 'listened in' to 'Jeffbyrne'. His deliberate procedure was not to monopolise, but to provide what he facetiously termed 'Platonics'. But Joyce seemed to prefer Byrne, unaccompanied, for those leisurely walks. We have since learned that in those years, 1902–1904, Joyce had commenced to outline a layout for his works of art and the Dublinised types he should select. To that end, who better than 'Jeffbyrne' who knew the Metropolis and its purlieus and sheebeens through and through and where Joyce could make personal contacts with his human material? Byrne was his trustworthy keeper.

I was to meet my friend Joyce in years later in unusual circumstances. In the twenties I was in Paris to watch Ireland playing France in a Rugby International. I rang Joyce and he asked me to come over to his flat. He seemed delighted to hear from me. When I arrived at the flat I discovered to my astonishment that he had been to see the match. 'How did you come to see the game, Joyce,' I said. 'I had to go and see the boys in green jerseys,' was his reply.

In 1931, I was again over in Paris, but this time as an Irish selector. Joyce must have guessed I was in town for the match because he phoned me to come around and see him. He had two tickets for the match and was going accompanied by an enthusiast. I was unable to go with Joyce, but agreed to meet him later. When I got around to see him eventually that evening, having dodged the after-match dinner, he told me that his eyes had not been strong enough to identify 'our team'. He rolled off the names of the Irish players who had taken part in the game and their respective clubs. Then to my astonishment he talked of prominent players in the 1923 side and added that he had attended the alternate games played in the intervening seasons whenever he happened to be in Paris. A substantial part of our conversation was taken up talking about the match and the players.*

I noticed that he still spoke with a good class Dublin accent. When I told him something that amused him on this occasion, he would break off into that famous Ha! Ha! Ha! cackle of his that I remembered so well from the time when he was a schoolboy. He was preoccupied with memories of Dublin. He enquired about my former house in Fitzwilliam Street, and the college boys who lived in the same line of houses. Then he

---

*   I have described in the introduction how subsequently Joyce sent Fallon copies of the avant-garde magazine *Transition*, which was serialising sections of what would later become *Finnegans Wake*. They seemed incomprehensible to Fallon, but, as it turned out, contained coded references to the match they both had seen in 1923.

invited me to check the accuracy after naming and numbering the households on both sides of that residential street in those far off years. He didn't overlook mention of a broad passageway that led to the residence and horse-training establishment of one Rogers, who, if we are to believe Joyce, wore 'leather leggins and a sports jacket day and night in mitigation of an iron-grey beard sprouting from a florid complexion'. (On my return to Dublin I checked Joyce's memory with the aid of a Thoms Dublin Directory, and found that he was correct in every item. At the same time I learned that the habit of listing a series of business names in shopping centres was one of Joyce's devices to retain pictures of his Dublin.)

'Do you remember,' he said, 'Fr. McArdle's catechism classes in "The Little House"? Fr. McArdle rounded the benches and fastening on to the shortcomings of two boys, the Farrell's I think it was, and having been satisfied that I knew our penny catechism of Catholic Doctrine better than anyone else, dispatched all three of us to a corner of the room for me to take on the role of teacher.'

He talked about Albrecht Connolly (this was the boy who had twisted Joyce's arm. In fact Joyce had been on much better terms with the Connollys than this incident would suggest). Albrecht was one of a talented family whose house was not far from Belvedere. He introduced Joyce to his widowed mother, brothers and sisters, and for a while Connolly's house was a second home for Joyce. I recall how I used to be puzzled why Mrs. Connolly would call Jim aside when we were all going home from school. We discovered later that she was taking Jim into the house to give him a meal. She knew of his difficult circumstances at home. One of Albrecht's sisters became a nun at the Loreto Convent. She had a clear recollection of Joyce, as I discovered when I visited her years later. She had been impressed by his imperturbability and precocious maturity as a young boy.

He had gone with Albrecht to visit her in the convent when he was in Dublin, and had also written to her from exile. She had taken a keen interest in his literary career and had followed the reviews of *Ulysses* and *Finnegans Wake* with avid interest. I bought her several of his early books including *Dubliners* and I remember the delight with which she received them.

Joyce's memory for detail on the occasion of my Paris visit was extraordinary. He recalled how he had exchanged whispers with the little Italian boy on his first day in Belvedere. He described our classroom with the crucifix over the fireplace, and listed, without hesitation, a score of the boys' names in our class; George Collins, Cassidy, Farrell, and others. We talked about the Wilkins boys with whom he had played Red Indians. Joe Wilkins, one of the boys, had later become a priest. Joyce seemed surprised at this. 'I never thought Joe would make a priest' was his comment.

He asked me to do 'Murphy'. By this he meant would I imitate our somewhat bucolic maths master at Belvedere. I impersonated for Joyce an incident when Murphy came into class looking somewhat the worse for the weather. Joyce had been sitting at the top of the class and said, 'You have a cold, sir?' Murphy muttered in his rich country voice, 'Thanks, that's only porter.' Joyce laughed at this, and I reminded him of the time I had played Ophelia to his Queen mother in the charade at Sheehy's house. When he was told of Ophelia's fate, Joyce had replied in a thick Dublin accent, 'Ah, the poor gerrul' (girl). He recalled other evenings he had spent at the Sheehy home. He could remember the names and occupations of everybody who attended these soirées.

I reminded him of the time three of us had accompanied him on a walk on Sandymount Strand. He strode out in front of us. I quoted from *Ulysses* and asked him was his description of the foul foreshore at Ringsend near the mouth of the Liffey taken from his experience on the walk that day:

'Unwholesome sandflats waited to suck his threading soles, breathing upward sewage breath.'

He made no comment; but instead fixed me with his medusoid stare. Apropos of this, he remarked that during his school days he had experimented in storywriting about happenings with persons of interest to him, and brought a few of them to George Dempsey for his comments . . .

As tactfully as I could, I questioned Joyce about his eyesight. His only comment was an irritated 'Ah', a long-drawn-out sigh containing undertones of frustration.

We decided to share a taxi, and I would drop him off at the eye clinic. He was concerned about my safety in Paris at that time of night, though I had no great distance to go. That was the last time I was to see him.

I felt that with all the changes success and fame had wrought in him, the James Joyce I had been talking to was not fundamentally different from the entertaining and brilliant companion I had known in our school days at Belvedere and later at University College.

PADRAIC COLUM

1881–1972

PADRAIC COLUM WAS born on 8 December 1881. His father was master of Longford workhouse but in the later part of his life came to live in Sandycove, Dublin, where Padraic grew up. While employed as a clerk, Colum wrote poetry and is counted among the notable dramatists and poets who were thrown up in the golden age of the Irish Literary Renaissance. Colum's friends included Yeats, Synge, Lady Gregory and James Stephens. His play *Broken Soil*, presented in the Abbey in 1905, was the first realist peasant play of the literary revival. His poems have been in almost every anthology: 'The Old Woman of the Roads', 'The Drover' and 'Cradle Song'. He also wrote the words of 'She Moves through the Fair', which was used as the theme song in the recent film on Michael Collins. Yeats wrote of the young Colum that 'he is a man of genius in the first gropings of his thought'. Colum emigrated to the United States in 1914 and with his wife Molly formed a duo on the faculty of Columbia University in New York. After her death he spent a number of months each year in his sister's home in Ranelagh where I used to meet him regularly in a small upstairs room filled with books and papers. When I was in New York I would go to his weekly evenings in his Manhattan apartment, which were attended by remnants of the literary and painting movements of the 1930s.

The last time I met him was in Deerfield, Massachusetts, in 1972 where he was in hospital. He was still lively enough to tell me a story about himself and George Moore in St. Stephen's Green, Dublin, arguing vociferously about Parnell and his mistress Kitty O'Shea. He was dead a few months later, the last survivor of the golden age of Irish literature.

WHEN I FIRST met James Joyce in 1901 or early in 1902, he was beginning to emerge as a Dublin 'character'. Already there was a legend about him.

That first meeting took place at one of Lady Gregory's evening parties. Seated in a corner were two young men whom I, who was about their age but had not been at the university, sized up as students. Now in Dublin at that time, students (they were mostly male) were thought of somewhat as they were in medieval times, as knowledgeable, profane, and, to a certain extent, detrimental. But these two were obviously not the ordinary run of students, since they were in a company (it would have been more fitting to say 'congregation') that included Lady Gregory and William Butler Yeats. Introduced to the two, I found I had heard their names before; they were Oliver Gogarty and James Joyce.

Each was already something of a celebrity. Oliver Gogarty, then a student at Trinity College, was known as an athlete – a bicyclist and a swimmer – as well as one to whom many of the scandalously witty sayings that were going the rounds of Dublin were attributed. The other's distinction was much less general. A year or two before that, when he was not much more than eighteen, James Joyce had achieved something that would have been gratifying to a writer twice his age; he had had an article published in the important *Fortnightly Review*. It was a review of Ibsen's *When We Dead Awaken*, for which the playwright, at that time the great master of European drama, later had William Archer, his English translator, express his appreciation to the young critic. It was a creditable article, one that showed erudition, loftiness of outlook, and, as one who read it thoughtfully could see, a dedication.

I do not remember that Joyce entered the conversation that evening. He and Gogarty sat apart, near the door, as if they did not quite belong at the gathering.

It may have been on this occasion that Lady Gregory asked Joyce to 'write something for our little theatre'. It was a request that the young author of *The Day of the Rabblement* was often to be derisive about. I don't know whether it was he or Gogarty who made up the limerick that is frequently quoted as Joyce's:

> There was a kind lady named Gregory,
> Who said: 'Come, all ye poets in beggary.'
> But she found her imprudence
> When hundreds of students
> Cried: 'We're in that ca-tegory.'

Several times after we were introduced at Lady Gregory's, Joyce and I came within recognizing distance on the street or in the National Library, but we had no communication. Joyce was aloof, and his blue eyes, perhaps because of defective vision, seemed intolerant of approach. He would enter the rotunda of the reading room generally between eight and nine o'clock in the evening. I won't say that he entered arrogantly, but he entered as one who was going to hold himself aloof from the collectivity there. Once, when I came to the counter after he had been there, an attendant said of a book that had been put aside, apparently to be reserved, 'For Mr. Joyce'. It was a book on heraldry.

Then, when Joyce and I were mentioned together as young poets, it was proper, I felt, that we should have some intimacy; this I decided one evening as we passed each other in the library. As he went through the turnstile on his way out, I went through too and spoke to him.

I think he took my approach as an act of homage (it was) and was willing to go along with me conversationally. We went out on Kildare Street and kept walking on, then along O'Connell Street until we turned toward where he lived. By this time Joyce was talking personally, or perhaps I should say biographically.

Looking back on that promenade, I know that I could have had no better introduction to the personality and the mind of that unique young man. He talked as a formed person talking to one whom he suspected of being unformed; he delivered, as he often did in those days, some set speeches. What maturity he had then!

It was natural to think, and I suppose I thought it, that a young man who distrusted, as he told me, all enthusiasms, was a singular character. And for Joyce to say this in the Dublin of the day was to set himself up as a heretic or a schismatic, and one who rifles the deposit of faith. I am trying to find a word for the way the young man standing on that street corner said, 'I distrust all enthusiasms'. It was not with any youthful bravado. It was rather like one giving a single veto after a tiring argument.

But it is not Joyce as the young man who separated himself from the rest of us, nor Joyce as the son of a Dublin personage, that I remember from that fortunate evening; rather it is Joyce as the maker of beautifully wrought poems. Joyce spoke his verse with deliberateness and precision, but in a naturally beautiful voice that had been cultivated for singing. The effect was more personal than in the case of AE or Yeats; it was Joyce exalted into the mode in which he knew himself free. 'The simple liberation of a rhythm'; this was his definition of the lyric at the time. I remember his rendering of lyrics that were favourites with him then – a rendering without the lilt that Irish poets are apt to give the verse they are repeating, one in which the poem became stylized speech (but with exceptional beauty of voice). I recall his reading of Ben Jonson's 'Still to be neat, still to be drest'; I remember, too, his rendering of Beatrice's song in the last act of *The Cenci* – 'False friend, wilt thou smile or weep, When my life is laid asleep?' And a lyric of Mangan, which even that poet's most devoted readers have passed over, became memorable when repeated by him: 'Veil not thy miror, sweet Amine.'

After this first talk with him, I did not see Joyce for some time. He left Dublin for Paris in the fall of 1902, stopping over in London to get some reviewing to do – the normal way for a young Dublin man of letters to cash in on his bookishness. Yeats was in London then and helped Joyce with introductions to editors.

He was away from Dublin for some months; then I heard that he had returned and later that his mother had died. I wrote a note of sympathy and received a formal acknowledgement. My family name has variant spellings, and when I wrote the note I used the one with the horrible 'b' at the end, a form that a grandparent quite mistakenly had used. The next time I saw Joyce he was standing despondently where there was a small company. In a distant way he said, 'I had a letter from you – or can it be there are two doves?' (In Latin, Irish, and French my name means that.) I mentioned the variations in spelling. 'And which do you use when your singing robes are about you?'

This was Joyce at his most detached. All of us used the cold approach from time to time, of course – the 'frozen mitt' was often proferred. Still, Joyce's attitude of ironic detachment toward me was not surprising. The nationalist group around *The United Irishman*, with which I was associated, was to him nothing more than 'the rabblement'. AE, whose Hermeticism he despised, was promoting whatever stock I had. Perhaps Joyce thought of me then as one of those whom he later described as:

> Those souls have not the strength that mine has
> Steeled in the school of old Aquinas.

But he seemed to be kin, at this stage, with his own 'comedian Capuchin'. The gestures he made with the ashplant he now carried, his way of making his voice raucous, were surely part of an act. And wasn't there, too, in his behaviour, the assertion of a young man conscious of his hand-me-down clothes, whose resort was the pawn office, and who was familiar with the houses in Nighttown? The raucous voice, the obscene limericks delivered with such punctilio . . . Was he playing Rimbaud? Villon?

It appeared that Joyce had brought back from Paris a cabaret song, 'Cadet Rousele', and would sing it at certain gatherings. So Oliver Gogarty had that name for him too: 'Have you seen Cadet Rousele?' The name suited the figure that, yachting cap on his head, tennis shoes on his feet, ashplant in hand, perambulated the streets of Dublin: Cadet Rousele. It was as though there were two projections of Joyce in those days, one his own person and the other the comic persons with which Gogarty invested him.

It was solely as a 'character' and that partly a Gogartian creation, that Joyce was known to Dubliners of that time. To himself, of course, he was altogether different; he had none of the approachableness, privately, of a 'character':

> That high, unconsortable one –
> His love is his companion.

But since the early Ibsen article he had written nothing, beyond the Mangan essay and a few lyrics shown to friends, so far as anyone knew. That he was an intellectually exceptional young man anyone who met him could tell, but they also knew he had frequently been in the gutter. There had been other brilliant young Dubliners who were now but fading 'characters'. Needless to say, no one foresaw *Ulysses* or *Portrait of the Artist* or even *Dubliners*.

About that time an early play of mine was produced by the National Theatre Society. Joyce asked me to let him see the script. I did. Afterward I encountered him in O'Connell Street, and he treated me to a private 'performance'. Pointing his ashplant at me, he said, 'I do not know from which of them you derive the most misunderstanding – Ibsen or Maeterlinck.' He had the script with him: the encounter must have been planned. It was in a roll, which permitted him to make its presentation to me significant. 'Rotten from the foundation up,' he said.

Joyce and Gogarty seemed to be engaged in some enterprise. An apostolate of irreverence! The rationalism of Catholicism and the non-rationalism of Protestantism; the nonsensicalness of Irish nationalism, the stupidity of British imperialism were satirized by them in verse and anecdote. What was creative was far from being let off. Joyce's ridicule of my play was to be expected, perhaps, but even Yeats was brought into mocking limericks. That the pair were collaborating on an anthology of inscriptions in public lavatories was known in their set and was regarded as a philosophers' divertissement.

Another time Joyce was among those in the National Library when I was; readers were departing. Timing my exit to be with Joyce's, who was at the turnstile with a friend, ready to leave, I left some volumes on the counter. They were *The World as Will and Idea*. When the three of us were on the stairway, Joyce said with the raillery he often used when addressing me in those days, 'You see before you – two frightful examples of the will to live.' Which meant that Joyce and his companion were out to pick up girls. The companion was taciturn, but I guessed it was he who knew the approaches. We went up Kildare Street and along Harcourt Street to the road off which I lived, the South Circular Road, which, with the lonesomeness of the canal banks adjacent, was a likely place for pickups. As we went along, Joyce talked in a way that was supposed to be a revelation to me of the uncloistered life. In those days he would have relished playing

Mephistopheles to Faust; later he was extremely fastidious in his conversation.

His mind mustn't have been totally preoccupied with prospects on the South Circular Road, for after we had cups of tea in a confectioner's in Harcourt Street and went strolling again, we shifted to the World as Idea. Ibsen, remember, was the avatar of the time. I spoke of having seen a non-professional performance of *A Doll's House* and of George Moore's saying to me at the end of it, 'Sophocles! Shake-speare! What are they to this!' Joyce's comment made the elder writer's seem filled with boyish enthusiasm. 'A postcard written by Ibsen will be regarded as interesting and so will *A Doll's House*.' But when we talked of *Hedda Gabler* Joyce showed his admiration for the Master while allowing me to say all the enthusiastic things.

Then he repeated in the original Norwegian a lyric of Ibsen about water lilies. His pronunciation of the words of the poem could not have been, I now realise, any better than that of a German with a few English lessons speaking a lyric of Shakespeare in the original. But as Joyce repeated the lines I had an image of floating flowers brought over into a verse music that I longed to match. The poem that I could never really know became for me a rhythmic challenge.

By this time we had reached the avenue that I lived on; I left the pair, who, as far as I could see, were still without prospects.

No matter how hungry or how shabbily he was dressed, he always had fine composure. His face with the blue eyes was resolved. He would repeat a lyric or a limerick, relate a

bawdy incident, or discuss a point in aesthetics in an unruf-
fled, deliberate way. Not even a compliment to his writing
could disturb him. Once, when I mentioned that I had read
an article of his, he replied in a way that was characteristic
of the matter and the manner of his speech: 'I received for it
thirty shillings which I immediately consecrated to Venus
Pandemos.'

One day Joyce came to me with a request for a loan of a
half-sovereign. A financial scheme was involved in its use. He
had been given a pawn ticket as a contribution to a fund he
was raising for himself. Now, to anyone else a pawn ticket
would be a minus quantity, but to Joyce it was realizable. The
ticket was for books, and six shillings was the amount they
were in for. As the ticket had been contributed by a medical
student, Joyce told me, the books were undoubtedly medical,
and so of value. And we would take them to our friend
George Webb on the Quay, and sell them, and make fifty or
even a hundred per cent on the transaction.

So we handed out the money, with its interest, at Terence
Kelly's pawnshop, and the books came across the counter to
us. Hastily we undid the wrappings. And lo and behold! the
books were an unsaleable edition of the Waverley Novels of
Sir Walter Scott, with one volume missing.

Sitting outside his shop, with his one closed and his one
open eye, George Webb received Joyce cordially. 'Some of
your Italian books, Mr. Joyce?' Joyce had taken Italian at University College, spoke it elegantly and fluently, and had picked
up a lot of valuable Italian books which he was selling at the
time. 'No, Webb; these are special,' replied Joyce. We opened

the parcel and exhibited the wretched set of romances. Very loftily indeed did Joyce talk to the most knowing bookseller in Dublin. 'But you have brought some Italian books with you, haven't you, Mr. Joyce?'

When he gathered that Joyce really wanted to sell him the books in the parcel, and that he had ransomed them from Terence Kelly's on the prospect of selling them, Webb had them wrapped up again for us. This most estimable of bookbuyers and booksellers, this George Webb of the swivel eye, was generally found seated meditatively outside his shelves and stacks; he mentioned quietly and firmly the price he would give or take. Across from him on the Quay was the shop of the black-bearded Hickey, who looked like a buccaneer rather than a bookseller, and who would come roaring out of the reaches of his shop, and beat you down if you wanted to sell, or would shamelessly boost the prices marked on the books on the stands outside if you wanted to buy. But George Webb was sympathetic to the book-wanter and the book-disposer. His fairness was recognized. If by chance and unknowingly you brought him the most sought-for book or pamphlet, say Shelley's *Address to the Irish People*, the price he offered you would be the proper price. Now he said mildly to us, 'Take the books back to Terence Kelly's; maybe you can get him to let you have back the six shillings.' We took them back and did manage to get our six shillings.

'I'm not like Jesus Christ – I can't walk on the water,' Joyce said to me the last time I saw him in the National Library. I won't go so far as to say that there was something desperate about him on this occasion, but he was putting on the air of a desperado. Raising funds for his journey to Zürich forced him into a sort of mendicancy. He spoke to me of approaching Lady Gregory. I expect he did, but if she helped him, she did it very privately; there is no mention of a gratuity to Joyce in her published correspondence.

Five years after he left Dublin I met the returned James Joyce in O'Connell Street. With him was a little boy, his four-year-old son, Giorgio. In appearance, bearing, manner, Joyce was improved. If I say he was more assured I may be misunderstood, for in one sense Joyce was always assured. But there is a difference between the assurance of a man who has only intellectual capital, and the assurance of a man who, besides that, has some sort of position. The Joyce I encountered in the street in 1909 had the assurance of position. He was no longer the 'character', the 'card', the 'artist' of Dublin conversation.

On this first of his visits back to Dublin, I found him as I had known him, or, if altered, a recognizable Joyce. One incident of this particular visit Joyce recalled affectionately, relating it to me years afterward. I remember it as illustrating the strong bond that was between him and his father, a bond of which one strand was music. The incident took place on an excursion made one afternoon by James Augustine Joyce and John Stanislaus Joyce – Stephen Dedalus and Simon Dedalus.

And so, after being five years apart, John Stanislaus Joyce and his son went into the country one afternoon, first taking a tram to the terminus at Terenure and walking to the outlying village of Rathfarnham. As they went along the quiet country road, the gossip of bars and committee rooms must have been poured into the ear of the author of *Dubliners* and the future begetter of *Ulysses*. A spacious saloon called The Yellow House, some way out into the country, was their terminus. In a big room, empty at the time, there were two pianos. Refreshment having been ordered, the older man sat at one. He played a theme that asked, 'Why did you go from us?' His son, 'Jim', at the other piano, played something in reply (he told me what it was, but I cannot remember). It was an epiphany of a sort, a showing forth of a relationship which was nearly always covered over, and Joyce dwelt on it later with some tenderness. There must have been something in his father that is not revealed in the speech of the Dublin 'character' so bent on 'jollifications'. John Stanislaus Joyce did not impose himself, as Irish fathers thought it was their bounden duty to do, on his son. There was a relationship, and it was not shown overtly, but, as on this occasion, in a very sensitive fashion.

Perhaps it was the day after his excursion with his father that I met James Joyce by appointment in Bewley's Coffee Shop in Westmoreland Street. Bewley's was the afternoon resort of the intelligentsia at that period; it was delightful for its mocha coffee, its freshly baked cakes with fresh butter. Joyce was there ahead of me; I came in with several books under my arm.

At a meeting of this kind Joyce was wont to remain aloof, leaving it to the other person to open up. The books I was carrying were collections of the work of Samuel Ferguson. His centenary was on, and I was writing about him for *Freeman's Journal*. I made an enthusiastic comment about one or two of the poems. Joyce picked up a volume, looking at the poem I mentioned, laid the book down, and like one resigned to his own disability said, 'I couldn't read this.' The suggestion was that he would have liked to.

Joyce reappeared in Dublin later in 1909, to give the city its first moving picture theatre. I had heard that there was an invention called the cinematograph, which produced continuously moving pictures, but its public functioning was unknown to me. Joyce was the first to explain it all to me, when, hearing he was again in Dublin, I arranged to meet him somewhere.

I was impressed when I stood with him inside the building that was being remodelled, and heard him give orders in Italian to the men at work. But I was troubled about one thing. Was this the site for a novel enterprise? Mary Street was on the verge of a slum area. Would people from the residential districts of Dublin come here? I had doubts. I supposed this was the only site available.

His friends did not see much of Joyce that second visit; he was out of Dublin, looking for theatre sites in Belfast and Cork, and when in the city he was busy supervising work in Mary Street, reporting back to Trieste, getting out publicity for this totally new enterprise. As regards the matter that was closest to his heart, the publication of *Dubliners*, that did not advance. The proofs that were to have been given to him shortly after his arrival were being held back. In the meantime, the Volta Theatre opened, Dublin saw its first cinema, and Joyce, with something outside his own private mission accomplished, went back to Trieste.

Suppose it had been otherwise? Suppose that when he

came back to Dublin this time Joyce had walked into the publishers' office and had been handed the proofs of his first book? Suppose he had gone back to Trieste, with a small cheque on a Dublin bank and a dozen copies of *Dubliners* in his trunk? What a different impression he would have had of his native city. Joyce would have been happier, of course; his mind would have been free of the suspicion of persecution he was prone to. But would there then have been a literature of exile?

The matter of *Dubliners* was still unsettled in the summer of 1912, when Joyce made another visit to Dublin. He spent an evening with my wife and me. Then we received a telegram saying that they were leaving Dublin for Galway that afternoon.

The Joyce whom I spoke to that last afternoon, when the only assistance I could offer him was the name of a man in London, was a Joyce now going into exile in earnest. True, he was going back to a city he had been at home in for a significant part of his life, where he had a wife and two children, not to speak of a brother and sister who had joined him there; he was going back to a place where there were people who were congenial to him. Why, then, did this particular departure come to be marked by him as an unmitigated exile? There is testimony that it was. Years afterward, with his friend the Triestine novelist, Italo Svevo, he was present at a performance of his play in London. '"Exiled"? I asked him,' says Svevo. 'Exiled. People who return to their home country.' 'But don't you remember,' said Joyce to me, 'how the prodigal son was received by his brother in his father's house. It is dangerous to leave one's country, but still more dangerous to go back to it, for then your fellow countrymen, if they can, will drive a knife into your heart.'

In 1923 my wife and I visited Paris. We called on Joyce at his home. I was curious, on that first visit, to see what changes his long stay away from Ireland had made in him. I noticed a Greek flag on the wall of the vestibule of his apartment. 'The Greeks have always brought me good luck,' he said when I looked enquiringly at it. The flag, he told me, was a relic of Trieste. In that Mediterranean seaport he had spoken to Greeks and learned the Greek vernacular. In Dublin, the then untravelled Joyce had spoken to me of the Greek epics as being outside European culture; he used to say that the *Divine Comedy* was Europe's epic. It must have been by the Mediterranean that he realised that the first artificer was a Mediterranean man, and it was then that Stephen Hero became Stephen Dedalus.

Our third visit to Paris, after the end of World War I, was in 1927, the fifth year of *Ulysses*. We saw more of Joyce this time than on the previous visit. Reminiscing with the composer of *Work in Progress*, I spoke of being in a Dublin music hall, the Lyric (or was it the Tivoli?), when a gang of students ragged a female performer by tossing at her feet a large corset. She made an indignant rejoinder, declaring that she was a Dublin girl and entitled to decent treatment from Dublin fellows. Maybe it was *because* she was a Dublin girl – residence might have set up a score against her – that there was the immodest demonstration. I didn't think that anyone except myself remembered it, and I remembered it because it was the first and last time I was among what was for me the far from respectable audience of that particular music hall. But Joyce hadn't missed it. With the triumph of a historian who has made a footnote to one of Gibbon's footnotes, he exclaimed: 'I have her in. She is the one who is mad jealous.' The performer's name was Madge Ellis. So there is it. And if I didn't make it public, would the best equipped commentator ever be able to reveal what is behind that 'madjealous' in *Finnegans Wake*?

Once Nora had decreed that 'Jim' was to get himself a new suit, and the three of us took a taxi to a shop near the Galeries Lafayette. Even while trying on pants and jackets under the scrutiny of his wife, Joyce was not completely detached from *Work in Progress*. He laughed like a schoolboy who has inserted a meaningful cipher on the margin of his lessons when I told him I had identified the 'Tantrist' of one of the instalments in *Transition*: he is Tristan the trickster, the one who leaps backward from Iseult's bed. 'I don't know how I can think of such things,' he said, as though delighted with himself.

One evening at dinner I listened to Joyce quote Goldsmith. That the author of *The Vicar of Wakefield* and *The Deserted Village* meant so much to the author of *Chamber Music* and *Ulysses* was something of a discovery.

I was later to make an even more interesting discovery. In the Arts Club, Dublin, a member, Mr. George O'Donnell, spoke to me about a book he had since his schooldays at Belvedere College, where he was a classmate of Joyce, on the front page of which Joyce had written a piece about him. He very kindly offered to lend me the book, and I have it before me now. It is *A Concise History of Ireland* by P. W. Joyce, published in 1894. The class in Belvedere had been reading Goldsmith's *Retaliation* and the sixteen-year-old Joyce singled out one of his classmates for an address that echoes Goldsmith's mock epitaphs. I believe it is the earliest piece of Joyce's verse that has been found:

G. O'Donnell

Poor little Georgie, the son of a lackey,
Famous for 'murphies' spirits, and 'baccy',
Renowned all around for a feathery head
Which had a tendency to become red.
His genius was such that all men used to stare
His appearance was that of a bull at a fair
The pride of Kilmainham, the joy of the class
A moony, a loony, an idiot, an ass.
Drumcondra's production, and by the same rule,
The prince of all pot boys, a regular fool.
All hail to the beauteous, the lovely, all hail
And hail to his residence in Portland gaol.

Joyce would become genial when he spoke of Goldsmith; he used to quote with enjoyment from *Retaliation* the lines about Burke:

Though fraught with all learning, yet straining his throat,
To persuade Tommy Townshend to lend him a vote.

He was unassuming, Joyce went on to say, praising Goldsmith for personal qualities. He spoke of it as virtue in a man to make no disturbance about what he does or the life he has to live. At that same dinner, a writer from whom Joyce was supposed to have inherited something – Jonathan Swift – was mentioned. As a Dublin man, if nothing more, Joyce might be expected to offer tribute to Swift. But all he said of him was, 'He made a mess of two women's lives.' When I remarked on Swift's intensity, Joyce said with quiet conviction, 'There is more intensity in a single passage of Mangan's than in all Swift's writing.' (We were all Irish at the table, and so the literary figures discussed were mainly Irish.) Though I could not agree with his estimate of Mangan – for Joyce it was highly extravagant – I was delighted that even now that he was a writer with a European reputation, he had kept his youthful admiration for a poet who is hardly known outside Ireland.

The talk went back to Irish writers. For Yeats's poetry Joyce had – but this was no news – a high regard; he mentioned that he had collaborated on a translation into Italian of *The Countess Cathleen*. Of course I remembered that a lyric from his play, 'Who will go drive with Fergus now?' had possessed the mind of Stephen Dedalus at a sorrowful time of his life.

Having spoken of Yeats, Joyce went on to speak of Synge and George Moore. He had also helped to translate Synge's *Riders to the Sea* into Italian. He said he thought the play too short to have a tragic scope. I disagreed with him in this, saying that in the stage production the keening of the women who come into the house gives it another dimension.

George Moore had given Joyce one of his recent books; he

was sorry it was not *Esther Waters*, which was the novel of Moore he admired. Other names came up as the company talked, Arthur Symons among them. Symons's translations of Verlaine, Joyce took it on himself to say, were equal to the originals.

Joyce and James Stephens were a great deal together about this time. We found this companionship a happy feature of the Joyce establishment during our sojourns in Paris. The author of *Ulysses* had come under the spell of the author of *The Crock of Gold*. And who wouldn't? No one in the world had so much spontaneity with so much gusto as James Stephens, so much wisdom with so much nonsense, so much fantasy with so much poetry.

If he had not been a poet and storyteller, James Stephens would have been a clown in the great style. I would see Joyce looking at him, as Stephens, with his brown eyes and his mobile face, was singing something about 'Mick Mulligan's terrier dog', and would guess a relationship between them that was different from the occult one that Joyce had announced, based on dates and names they had in common. They had an occupational relationship, I thought then, they were both of the company of a group of strolling players. I could see them in a booth or on a stage in the open air, one appearing and singing some great aria, then the other coming on with a monologue composed of poetry and fantasy. What a performance that pair could give!

Joyce's attachment to Stephens was shown by a retort that came from him when I questioned something that Stephens had done. He and Cynthia had left Paris to be house guests of Lady Londonderry. 'Isn't it a wonder,' I said to Joyce, 'that James Stephens would have anything to do with a descendant of Castlereagh?' Joyce did not answer for a moment: then he said with some rancour, 'Haven't I seen you talking with John Dillon's son?'

I will have to explain why the retort was a staggering surprise to me. Lord Londonderry was a descendant of the Castlereagh who, in the most cynical fashion, destroyed the Irish Legislature. John Dillon belonged to the group in Parnell's party that deposed him as leader. In Joyce's time and mine, John Dillon, backed by an Irish constituency, worked for the restoration of the Legislature. That Joyce should put John Dillon and Castlereagh in the same class was inexplicable to me. John Dillon's son was in Paris; he was a philologist studying Sanskrit and the connections of Old Irish with it. My wife and I had brought this young man, Myles Dillon, to Joyce's, and Joyce had treated him with his usual courtesy. And all the time he was remembering that he was entertaining the son of a man who had helped to bring about the downfall of the Uncrowned King!

Pondering on this, I found something magnificent in the unreason of Joyce's loyalty to an individual who had stirred his imagination. What passion a boy of ten or eleven must have known as he watched Parnell's downfall! Was it this that separated him from all political interests? 'Colum, this is the second time I have come into the room and found you talking politics,' he once admonished me.

About this time I wrote an essay on Joyce for *The Dublin Magazine*. Here is how I saw him. He was approaching fifty.

Slender, well made, he holds himself very upright; he is tastefully dressed, and wears a ring in which there is a large stone. The pupils of his eyes are enlarged because of successive operations, but his gaze is attentive and steady. There is a small tuft of beard on his chin. The flesh of his face has softness and colour – the glow that a child's face has. A detail: his hands have now the softness, the sensitivity, of a man who has to depend a good deal on touch. All the lines of his face are fine; indeed his appearance is not only distinguished but winning. This appearance and his courtesy give him great dignity. Then when one takes note of his appearance one perceives that neither his head nor his forehead is large; the forehead with three deep lines graven on it is narrow, the well-shaped head is small. But head and forehead curve upward and outward, giving a sense of fullness and reasonance, each suggesting instrumental amplitude. The jaws close to the chin make the face triangular; they too suggest something in which there is sound. The abundant hair, brushed backward, has lines in it that are like strings, like iron-gray strings.

One evening at dinner the talk turned on saints, but Joyce would have none of them except St. Patrick. He dismissed Saint Francis. He declared he took little interest in Augustine. Aquinas, then, whose aesthetic the young hero of *Portrait of the Artist* promoted? Joyce would have none of the great Doctor either, or of Saint Ignatius, despite his Jesuit training. The only saint he would praise was Saint Patrick; him he vaunted above all the other saints in the Calendar. 'He was modest, and he was sincere,' he said, and this was praise indeed from Joyce. And then he added: 'He waited too long to write his *Portrait of the Artist*' – Joyce meant Saint Patrick's *Confession*.

After dinner Joyce sang a tragic and colourful country song I have never come across in any collection nor heard anyone else sing. It is about a man who has given his wife to a stranger – he may be from Fairyland, he may be Death himself. Joyce learned this song from James Stephens.

> I was going the road one fine day,
> Oh, the brown and the yellow ale!
> And I met with a man who was no right man;
> O love of my heart! And he said to me,
> 'Will you lend me your love
> For a year and a day, for a year and a day?'
> Oh, the brown and the yellow ale,
> The brown and the yellow ale.

Those refrains in Joyce's voice had more loss in them than I have ever heard in any other singer's. He once said to me, 'A voice is like a woman – you respond or you do not; its appeal is direct.' He said this to show that what was sung transcended in appeal everything that was written. His own voice in the humorous and the sorrowful songs was unforgettable.

In December of 1931 Joyce's father, John Stanislaus Joyce, died in Dublin. He had done little, as a father, for his eldest son – in fact he had done nothing – but Joyce cherished his image and the memory he had of the musical, sporting, irresponsible, entertaining man. A few years after the publication of *Ulysses* Joyce had commissioned a Dublin artist, Patrick Tuohy, to paint a portrait of his father. The old man lived on a realized insurance with perhaps an old-age pension. Like many old men in Dublin who had some sort of position, he lived not in a lodging house, or a boarding house, but with a family, which, in those days, could let him have board and room for twenty-five or thirty shillings a week.

Not long after John Stanislaus's funeral, I happened to be going from Paris to Dublin, and Joyce asked me to call on the family with whom his father had roomed. It was his hope, I think, that I would bring back some remembrance of the man on whom Simon Dedalus in *Portrait of the Artist* was based. I wrote to the head of this family when I got to Dublin, telling him I'd like to see him and talk about his late tenant. I had intended to visit him, so that I could get some impression of John Stanislaus's last surroundings, but instead he came to see me.

He was a nice young man who gave the impression that in his domicile the old man had been taken care of, but as he talked about him, the emphasis was on the effort he and his wife had made to keep him decently. To him John Stanislaus Joyce was a battered, shabby old person who had come to live with them after some kind of a breakdown – either an accident such as befalls old men or a shock that had left him somewhat astray. The young man knew that his tenant had meant something to the outside world, for a portrait painter had been in to put him on canvas, and a newspaperman to interview him, but the John Stanislaus whom his son wanted to hear about had never existed for this young Dubliner.

So my report, when I got back to Paris, was disappointing, and I think I, as its bearer, was disappointing, too, to Joyce. Here was I in an apartment that had on the wall Tuohy's *Portrait of a Dublin Gentleman* and other portraits of men and women of his family. And I was making my report to one for whom the tradition of gentlemanliness was important.

Joyce and I went for walks together, Joyce sometimes silent, sometimes conversing. I realized how tragically lonely great fame can leave a man. But I also remember oddities of discourse on these promenades. Why did Joyce have to be abusive about nuns? Why did he think that nuns ranked with tailors in a sort of nullity? He reminded me: 'They have no office in the Church. They can't even assist at Mass like altar boys.' He did not mention that one of his sisters was a nun. She was in a convent in New Zealand, and from what I heard from one who had visited her, she had an affection for James; for she kept as a relic the surplice he wore as a boy when he served at Mass. (The mention of Joyce as an acolyte reminds me that no exegete has noticed in his prose the cadences of the Latin responses to the celebrant, broken by the ringing of a bell in an unfilled chapel.) A priest among passers-by drew a favourable comment from Joyce on the garb of French priests. They wore soft hats. 'If somebody would kidnap the silk hats of the priests in Ireland, wouldn't that be a gain for the Church?' he remarked.

Then came Munich, and a shamefaced relief was evident, at least at first, among the sojourners in Paris. The Joyces came back to the city. When Joyce telephoned me, he mentioned the settlement. 'Give him Europe?' he said angrily. At this time Joyce was instrumental in trying to place some relatives of a Jewish friend of his, Herr Brauchbar, whom he had known in Trieste. Brauchbar had been helpful to Joyce. Joyce did not forget it. As a result of Joyce's pleading, I wrote to the Minister of Justice in Ireland. After initial setbacks, Herr Brauchbar's relative was permitted to take up residence in Ireland.

In Paris, my wife and I had our last dinner with the Joyces. As the evening drew to a close, Joyce was able to distract his wife's attention while he got the waiter to bring him another bottle of white wine. I conducted him downstairs and had him back and at the table in time to finish his wine before Nora, who had also retired, reappeared. She found him standing before the bowing waiters, whom as usual he had tipped extravagantly.

We were obliged soon afterward to leave Paris for New York. We had boarded the boat train when, looking out of the window, we saw Joyce and Nora coming along the platform.

'Good-bye, Joyce! Luck to *Finnegans Wake*,' we called. As the train began to move, Joyce, stumbling on a bit, said to my wife, 'We don't want you to go, but anyhow, you'll be safe in America.'

Arthur Power

1895–1985

A n Anglo-Irish gentleman whose family house was Bellevue, Co. Waterford, Power was from an old Catholic family who had not conformed but kept their lands during the Reformation. He was educated at an English public school. Many of the members of his family had been in the army, and Arthur fought in the cavalry at Ypres in the First World War until he was invalided out in 1916. After the war he went to live in Paris where he wrote for the *New York Herald*. He became friendly with the painters Modigliani and Maillot, and under their influence he began to paint. He became a close friend of Joyce, who confided in him, fascinated perhaps by the agile, inquisitive mind of this Anglo-Irish Catholic landed gentleman who wanted to be an artist.

Power returned to Ireland in the 1930s where he set up an art gallery in Balfe Street, Dublin, and contributed art criticism to the *New York Herald*. He lived in a charming Georgian villa on Park Avenue, Sandymount, just a few minutes from the sea. There I would visit him regularly for many years and try to persuade him to redo his papers so that his conversations with Joyce could be put into readable form.

When in 1966 Giorgio Joyce came to Dublin, Power invited me to have tea with him in the garden. I sat with the butterflies flitting between apple blossom and sweet laburnum listening enthralled to the two as they talked. Giorgio was over six feet tall and well built, and he spoke English in a way that Italians sometimes do, with a quaint mixture of Edwardian slang. He had sung in opera and had a fine baritone voice. His hero was John MacCormack, the internationally famous Irish tenor.

'John MacCormack is a corker,' Giorgio said.

'Oh no, I can't bear him,' said Power.

Giorgio then started to sing 'Il Mio Tesoro' from *Don Giovanni* in MacCormack fashion. He even rendered McCormack's famous prolonging of the *cercate* (which so impressed the audience at La Scala) in which the phrase following is reached without taking a breath. The more he expounded on his hero's virtuosity, the more agonised Power's face became till he put his hands over his ears, saying, 'No, no, I can't bear it.'

Later I was to visit Giorgio in Zürich where he lived with his wife, Asta Jahnke-Osterwalder, an ophthalmologist. I had persuaded the then Taoiseach Jack Lynch to authorise a state funeral for James Joyce, if Giorgio would consent to the body being taken back to Ireland by naval corvette, as had happened in 1948 when W.B. Yeats's remains were returned from France.

Giorgio was hugely enthusiastic about the proposal and asked me for a letter from the Taoiseach to put the matter on a formal basis. I was able to forward this to him. But his health was not good and I sensed that his wife was not keen for her husband to get involved in the stress of a public event of this kind. Giorgio died shortly after and the project lapsed.

Arthur Power, in the second half of his life, did many very beautiful paintings in pastel form. His cubist portrait of Joyce is a clever comment on the author of *Finnegans Wake*. He died in the British military hospital in Foxrock in 1985.

LIKE HIS HERO Ulysses, Joyce was a man of many habitations. When I met him first he was living in a gloomy iron-shuttered flat in the Boulevard Raspail. In the centre of the sitting-room was a huge red lampshade spread out like a flounced petticoat, while in the corner my attention was attracted to a collection of sickly yellow plants, wondering if the last tenant had left them as a legacy to the unfortunates who were to follow him. However, one discovered that Joyce attached great importance to them. 'They are phoenix palms,' he told me, 'and remind me of the Phoenix Park, but I cannot keep them alive in this damned brothel,' he added mournfully while I gazed in mute amazement at the author's all embracing imagination. This was the first occasion I had visited Joyce at home; but it was not my first meeting with him. That had taken place at the Bal Bullier, a famous dance hall opposite the café of the 'Closerie de Lilas'.

On the evening in question I had gone there to meet a party which, however, did not materialize; and I wandered about the hall watching the couples dancing, thinking perhaps I might meet someone I knew to dance with. I saw a group of people at the far end of the hall I knew, but I did not want to get in with them, I wanted to dance; life is too short to talk it away. However, towards the end, one of the ladies hailed me over, and introducing her friends who sat at the table, presented me to James Joyce.

I liked the man; slight and gracefully built, with a rather Shakespearian head, he wore strong glasses, which greatly magnified one eye. A small goatee beard covered a thin-lipped, curiously shaped mouth. His hands were noticeably fine, and slight fingered. Everything of him proclaimed a poet – everything except his mouth. His manner was sympathetic rather than friendly – because Joyce's social manner was not easy. He surrounded himself normally with a kind of mental barbed wire – but his exquisite manners were reminiscent of the Dublin of the Grand Days. That remarkable Irish courtliness, he always had. And the more difficult the position was the more perfect was his manner. It had the detachment and nobility to it of a grandee, and was as superior as a diamond is to glass to what passes for manners among provincial gentry and nobility. It was the outward sign of inward refinement; and like all remarkable men he had no conceit; no boorish arrogance.

He asked me if I was 'a man of letters'. The question 'man of letters' had a curiously old-fashioned nineteenth-century tang to it; in the rough and tumble of a popular dance hall it sounded like an invitation to a minuet if only an intellectual one. I told him I was interested but did little myself.

'What are you trying to write?' he asked.

I told him that I was interested in the eighteenth-century French satirists, and I wanted to write like them.

'You'll never do it,' he said, 'never – you are an Irishman – you must write in an Irish tradition; write what is in your blood, and not what is in your head.'

I told him I was tired of nationality. I wanted to become international – all great writers were international.

'Yes – but they were national first – if you are sufficiently national you will be international.'

We rose to go out, and I gathered that the party was to celebrate the fact that an American publisher, a Miss Beach, had agreed to publish his new book, *Ulysses*. He had spent seven years writing it, in Trieste, in Zürich, in Paris; and having it written, he had had no idea who would undertake its publication. Now Miss Beach had agreed to do it. We stopped for a while at the Café des Lilas, on the high terrace facing the miniature wood which fills that corner of the boulevard, and drank 'tilleuls' before returning home. Joyce spoke of the power of language; and he compared the English language to an organ for its sonorous wealth. Several of us protested that we preferred the French language for its precision and musical quality. But he would not agree, and to support his argument he quoted passages of the English Bible, and then quoted corresponding passages out of the French text.

Joyce had a marvellous memory, and he could quote stanzas of poetry on end. To support his argument now he quoted passages from the Authorized Version.

'And He came and touched the bier, and they that bore him stood still. And He said: "Young man, I say to thee, arise."'

'Et s'étant approché, il toucha la bière, et ceux qui la portaient s'arrêtèrent, et il dit: "Jeune homme, je te dis, lève-toi."' And Joyce compared the weakness of 'Je te dis, lève-toi' with – 'I say unto thee, arise' . . . and he went on to compare two longer passages, for Joyce was nothing if he was not thorough, out of Matthew, quoting the English version first:

'Whereof if thy right hand or thy foot offend thee, cut them off, and cast them from thee; it is better for them to enter life halt or maimed rather than having two hands or two feet to be cast into everlasting fire.'

And then the French version.

'Que si ta main ou ton pied te fait tomber dans le pêche, coupe les: et jette les loin de toi; car il vaut mieux que tu entres boiteux ou manchot dans la vie, que d'avoir deux pieds ou deux mains, et d'être jeté le feu éternel.'

He remarked how superior in language, in music, and strength, was the English version to the French.

It was an argument in which one required a very good memory so as to be able to quote numerous and similar passages in the two languages, and none of us was equal to it; so we relinquished it, leaving the palms of victory with him, but secretly holding to our own opinion as in all arguments between opposing ideas.

After that I did not see him for some time. The next flat I visited him in was in the Avenue Charles Floquet. This, in contrast, was a fine airy apartment, and the most attractive of his many habitations. It looked out on to the Eiffel Tower opposite, and since it was near the Ecole Militaire through the trees one occasionally caught glimpses of uniformed officers riding past in the Parc du Champs de Mars.

But unfortunately Joyce's eyes were very bad at that time, and as likely as not when one entered one would find him lying on a bed, the blinds drawn, stooping his eyes in the darkened room, when he would wisecrack that he was 'waiting for Ireland's Eye to do its duty'.

Then towards evening he would get up, when I would accompany him down town in a taxi to his occulist Dr. Borach who had his consulting rooms in the Rue de la Paix. Going up a private back stairs we would wait in a small, badly papered room evidently reserved for V.I.P.'s. Presently, after a time Dr. Borach, a soft-looking, silent-moving man, who looked as though he had never taken a draught of fresh air in his life, would enter in a hurry, examine Joyce's eyes with a lens, make a few remarks, and tell him to call again in two days time. Then we would descend those narrow back stairs again, and hailing a taxi, drive to the Café Francis. This café looked across the Seine and faced the ornate Pont de l'Alma supported by those famous sculpted Zouaves, which also act as hydrometres in the temperamental Seine and warn Parisians of possible inundations.

This café was a favourite haunt of Joyce's at this time, and here he would drink a Cinzano-à-l'eau, its rich ruby colour being more evocative than its alcoholic content, and discuss Irish literature, Dublin, and the disadvantages of possessing a Celtic temperament. After a while we would return to the flat where Mrs. Joyce would provide an excellent dinner, chicken cooked in wine being a 'spécialité de la maison'.

Indeed some of my happiest memories are of sitting down to this family meal with his son, the foreign-mannered and dapper Giorgio, just coming to be a young man, and the young Lucia, silent and sensitive, but gay nevertheless, and with no shadow of the subsequent tragedy which was to fall so unexpectedly on her.

And if report has it that in Dublin, Trieste, and Pola, Joyce had been wild and uncontrollable in his youth, when his friend Alessandro Francini would find him lying almost senseless in the gutters of the città vecchia of Trieste, now he gave the impression of being calm and settled, confident even; that is, as confident as he ever was, for strangely enough his confidence was inclined to ebb and flow with the tides of his temperament. For though he had braved and flaunted all accepted social and literary conventions in that great scoffing book of his, yet at times, it seemed, that like all sensitive men he would secretly query the ultimate value of his talent, his spirit weakening for the moment under the blast of an adverse criticism, perhaps; or from some secret psychological cause. It is something which others have noticed also. To my mind, anyway, it was one of the most attractive and human things about him, when collapsing on a seat with those much magnified eyes fixed questioningly on you he would repeat some malicious criticism he had read. The one which seems to have affected him most was the statement that he was a middle-class writer, whatever that may mean, but which in the pre-war world of fascism sounded like the threatening beat of a drum.

But on meeting him a few days later one would know by the gleam in his eye and the way he turned his head that his confidence – his superconfidence, in fact – in his talent had returned.

Also, I think that he felt sure that in Paris – the last of the human cities as he described it – when his work came to be published it would be more appreciated than anywhere else. Intellectually Paris is a city without prejudice, whatever its current political ferment might be. At that time the atmosphere, owing to the continual hargle-bargle going on over reparations, was, as often as not, violently anti-British. So intense was it at times that it met you like a wave when you went out into the street; for French emotionalism can run swift and high.

But already during his short stay he had made a number of friends and staunch adherents such as Pound, Miss Beach, and the French writers Gide and Valery Larbaud.

Indeed Larbaud was so enthusiastic that on reading some extracts from the courageous American *Little Review*, as well as the typescript of *The Oxen of the Sun*, which Miss Beach had sent him, he wrote to her, 'I am raving mad over *Ulysses*. It is as great, comprehensive, and human as Rabelais,' adding that since he had read it he had been unable to write, or sleep; he proposed to translate some pages to go with an article on the author in the *Nouvelle Revue Française*, at that time the most influential literary magazine in France.

One of the many things which intrigued French writers, and in fact the writers and intellectuals of all nations alike, was that Joyce's book was based on Homer's *Odyssey*, his hero's adventures, if you can call Bloom a hero, paralleling those of the wily Greek king. I remember once, for instance, how he compared the barmaids in the Ormond Hotel and the Sirens, saying that the barmaids were fine only to the waist with a careful hair-do, and make-up, and fresh, well-laundered blouses, but below the waist they were fish-tailed, wore dirty old skirts, rough mended stockings, and broken comfortable shoes, all which were not seen, of course.

So the analogy is worked out from chapter to chapter, starting with the Telemachus Episode in the Martello Tower at Sandycove; to the Nestor in Mr. Deasy's school; the Proteus, 'the old man of the sea' in the Sandymount Strand episode; The Sirens in the Ormond bar and 'sonnez-la-cloche'; and on to the final episode of Penelope in which, according to Vico's philosophy, a semi-goddess is shrunk to normal size.

Indeed, on meeting Joyce himself one could not but be reminded that his wandering existence was similar to that of his chosen hero, travelling as he had done from country to country and from town to town; and now in Paris from flat to flat, and from hotel to hotel, to say nothing of his numerous departures down into the French countryside to Nice, Burgundy, Brittany, and even into Holland and Switzerland; always restless, and always seeking. Indeed I remember him telling me on his return how while he had been staying down at Chartres he had listened with relish one evening to the conversation of some local women as they had washed the clothes against the stones in the river, a conversation which he later incorporated into the famous monologue of 'Anna Livia Plurabelle'.

'Tuck up your sleeves and loosen your talk-tapes. And don't butt me – hike! – when you bend. Or whatever it was they threed to make out he thried to two in the Fiendish park. He's an awful old reppe. Look at the shirt of him! Look at the dirt of it!'

As we know, he finally placed the scene, as he placed everything, back in Dublin – this Dublin which he never left in his imagination, and which he had hated and even despised in his tormented youth, but which after long exile he had re-found to cherish; now a sort of half-real and half-dream city; for Dublin was to Joyce what Florence was to Dante, the city of his soul.

Another novelty about *Ulysses* which intrigued contemporary writers was what he called his 'telegraphic style'; short pungent sentences which he considered the proper ones for the present day; a sort of literary infra-red ray in which he figured everything as in a cubist picture, even to the very larva of life.

'Ulysses is not a hero' – a priest had said to him at Clongowes. But Joyce thought he was, on his own terms, for he had always admired this wily wanderer who had surmounted his difficulties with determination and cunning; as stoically as *Ulysses* Joyce had condemned himself for years to such thankless tasks as keeping books, teaching, and working in a bank rather than sell his talent, suffering from the continual snubs and frustrations of publishers but never losing sight of his ultimate purpose, constantly carrying this image of Dublin with him wherever he went, determined once and for all to break down the classical and romantic image which had dominated literature for so long.

It was the medieval and the medievalists which attracted him most. I remember one day walking with him down the Boulevard St. Michel. On our left rose the spire of the Sainte Chapelle with that angel poised on its summit which always seems just to have alighted; while further down was the ancient Monastery of the Cluny, and those huge and sinister hulks of masonry, the remains of the original wall of Paris. 'It was the true spirit of Europe,' he said; 'think of the magnificent civilization we would have had if we had remained in that tradition.' He looked on the Renaissance and its return to Classicism as a return to intellectual boyhood. 'Compare,' he continued, 'a medieval building with a classical one, Notre Dame with La Madelaine, for instance; Notre Dame with plane countering plane, roof against roof, its flying buttresses, and erupting gargoyles.' He maintained that the present age was gradually returning to medievalism, remarking finally, with some bitterness, that if he had lived in the fourteenth or fifteenth century he would have been much more appreciated.

Also the Ireland he had known, in his opinion, was still medieval, and Dublin a medieval city in which the sacred and the obscene jostled shoulders.

'Show a Renaissance work to an Irish peasant,' he exclaimed, 'and he gazes at it in cold wonder, for it is not his world'; he would point out how Yeats was a typical medievalist with his interest in magic, his Countess Cathleens, and his belief in signs and symbols, and his later bawdiness . . . 'And it is this which separates an Irishman from Englishmen, Frenchmen, Italians, and from the rest of Europe, for we have never been subjected to the Lex Romanus, nor are we Renaissance men.'

I remember when talking to him in Paris once I was explaining my uncertainty as to what creative lines to proceed upon, amid all the confusing and, it seemed, jarring claims of Modernity. He recommended study of the *Book of Kells*. 'Wherever I have been,' he said, 'in whatever pass of life, or circumstances, I have always carried that with me and gone to it for inspiration. You can compare much of my work to the intricate designs of its illuminations, and I have pored over its workmanship for hours at a time in Dublin, in Trieste, in Rome, in Geneva – wherever I have been, and I have always got inspiration from it.'

Also when talking about literature he maintained that a country must be vintaged before it could produce literature –

in other words, it must have an odour . . . 'The first thing you notice when you visit a country is its smell, and in literature Rabelais smells of Medieval France; Chaucer of the England of the Middle Ages; Don Quixote of Spain; and *Ulysses* smells of the Dublin of my day.'

'It certainly has an effluvia,' I told him.

'Yes, it smells of Anna Liffey – not always a sweet smell but a pungent one all the same.'

'Also,' he remarked, 'you must remember that we are an uninhibited race, seldom behaving or thinking as convention demands.' He quoted Bernard Shaw as a typical example. 'Restraint is irksome to us, and that is what gives us our originality; had we been allowed to develop our own Celtic civilization instead of this mock English one imposed on us, and which has never suited us, think of what an original interesting civilization we might have produced. Indeed, it is my revolt against the English conventions, literary and otherwise, that is the main source of my talent.'

Also talking of writing, he said that he did not believe in planning it all beforehand on the classical formula, for, as he said, 'the good thing comes in the writing – words create', or, to use the French imagist poet Mallarme's phrase – 'leave the initiative to them'.

But, on the other hand, he believed in writing dangerously. 'For Classicism is dead,' he declared. 'It was the art of the gentlemen, and gentlemen are out of date.'

Another very important issue with him, and for which he suffered much, was the liberation of literature. English-speaking puritanism had restricted the freedom of the author, the freedom they had had on the Continent for centuries. This he was determined to break down, and because he flouted the Anglo-Saxon conventions he was prosecuted, banished, and finally burnt as a heretic in a kind of intellectual auto-da-fé. But he looked on himself as in the tradition of writers like Chaucer, Brantome, Rabelais, Maupassant, and others. Yet I think it was something that made him shy and diffident in company, for I remember him saying to me, 'You know there are people who would refuse to sit in the same room with me.'

As we know, the printers in England refused to print his book, and the editors of the *Little Review* in America were prosecuted and fined, even though two of the judges had to admit publicly that the particular passages read to them were incomprehensible. And it was Miss Beach who finally agreed to print and publish *Ulysses* in France with Darantiere, a friend of Mlle. Mounier's. That party at the Bal Bullier, where I had first met Joyce, had been the occasion to celebrate the signing of the contract between them.

After this I did not see him for some time (being away in Ireland most probably), and when we did meet again he was staying in a hotel close to the Gare Montparnasse. When I entered the hotel room where he was, I found him lying on the bed with the blinds drawn, surrounded by a collection of half-written manuscripts, undergoing one of his difficult periods, miserable in soul and body. Indeed, one could not help wondering how he could work under these conditions; a lift continually grinding up and down outside his door; the noise and bustle of luggage being wheeled along the passage outside; a child crying in the next room; but persisting as he had always persisted! Yeats's lines from 'Nineteen Hundred and Nineteen' came to me:

> O man in his own secret meditation
> Is lost amid the labyrinth that he has made
> In art or politics.

However, apart from his eye trouble, I need not have commiserated with him, for he told me that he preferred to work surrounded by activity – 'honest to God activity', as he remarked pointedly, and that he had found it impossible to work in the silence and security of that room especially designed for writing, which Larbaud had lent him, near the Luxemburg Gardens; a room I once visited with him to collect some manuscripts. Built in the foundations of a house it was fashioned like the bunk on a ship with a long table down the centre. Cool in summer; owing to its small size it could easily be heated in winter, and it had seemed to me ideal in every way. But its very noiselessness had made it impossible for him to work there.

However, he did not remain much longer in this hotel, for shortly afterwards he had to undergo yet another operation from the ever ready hands of Dr. Borsch, when he entered the clinic in the Rue du Cherche Midi. Here I visited him, lying in a small low-ceilinged room with one single dim light burning over his bed. Its general dilapidated appearance surprised and dismayed me, belonging as it did to a leading occulist, conditions which prompted Joyce to compose the following verse:

The clinic was a patched one,
Its outside old as rust
And every place beneath that roof
Lay four feet thick in dust.

But what worried him most of the time was that he thought that with its constant use he had contracted Atropine poisoning. He asked me to hunt up a book for him on the subject, fearing as he did the effect it might have on his brain. But when I called again with a book on poisons borrowed out of the American library, someone had forestalled me with a small library on the subject.

In the meantime, Mrs. Joyce had been hunting for a suitable flat which at last they found at 2 Square Robiac in a cul-de-sac running off the rue de Grenelle not very far from the former Charles Floquet; here he remained for seven years, longer than in any other place; here they had their own furniture, and at last he was able to install his family pictures which with Celtic reverence he had carried all round Europe; old-fashioned Georgian portraits by Comerford of Cork, of serious and respectable looking women wearing big bonnets tied under the chin. One which I particularly remember was of a fine-looking old gentleman in a red hunting coat and a white stock, a relation of Daniel O'Connell, so Joyce said – all these have since been lost when his effects were sold up by the landlord during the war to pay the rent – portraits which breathed of country houses, farmlands, horses, tea-parties, visits to fairs and to church; the usual country round of succession and tradition out of which had unexpectedly risen this light-limbed rebel.

It is this flat which one associates with him more than any

other, perhaps because he lived in it for so long, and it was the one in which I visited him most constantly.

Also at the time he decided that he wanted to have his father's portrait painted in Dublin to add to the collection, and asked me to recommend an artist. I suggested Paul Henry, Leo Whelan and others, but he did not respond. Then the name of Patrick Tuohy occurred to me. 'Yes,' he said – deciding on the moment – 'I think I know his father, Doctor Tuohy – I will have him do it' – a queer touch of provincialism, so it seemed to me at the time.

However, when it arrived it turned out to be a very good portrait of the old reprobate sitting in his armchair with his tugged moustache and fierce rheumy eyes, all Dublin's gossip bubbling on his broken lips – Ulysses incarnate.

Then Tuohy came over to Paris to paint the entire Joyce family. But his personality irritated Joyce so that when Tuohy talked to him about painting his soul, Joyce answered him shortly, 'Don't worry about my soul, but get my tie straight.' Also he asked him point blank once – 'Do you want to paint me, or my name?'

And every time one went into the flat one was sure to find Tuohy at all hours sitting on the floor checking one of his portraits in a mirror. In fact he seriously upset the rhythm of Joyce's life. Also, he was inclined to irk Joyce in annoying ways, jibing that he should now write 'a best seller'.

But Tuohy was mentally a sick man, for he confided to me that he had an ulcer on his palate which was eating into his brain. I suggested he should consult a doctor. 'They are no use,' he answered me hopelessly.

After his stay in Paris, Tuohy went to America to the Southern States, and then moved up to New York, where one day, poor fellow, he pasted up his studio with newspapers and turned on the gas. When I told Joyce of his death he replied coldly, 'He nearly made me commit suicide too' – a remark of unusual bitterness for him.

Another picture he had in his flat was Vermeer's picture of Ghent, of the river flowing past the quays lined with those quaint red brick houses which, like *Ulysses*, was a picture of a city, and so had a particular significance for him. But in general he was not much interested in art, for like many other writers, I think, he regarded it as inferior, and I remember as we walked down the narrow Rue du Seine with the buses roaring behind our backs, I used to stop before the picture dealers' windows and point out the latest Braque or Modigliani trying to raise his enthusiasm. But after looking at them for a while he would only ask 'How much are they worth?' which I am certain was intended for a sarcasm.

Indeed, not only did he appear not to be interested in modem art, then the rage in Paris, but he also ignored the multiple artistic activity that went on around him. The Russian Ballet for instance . . . *Parade* . . . *Caisse Noisettes* . . . and Stravinsky's electric *Sacre du Printemps* in which the movement of the dancers was like that of a rugby scrum when, at the end, a single figure emerges to dance the pas-seul of Spring.

Indeed at one of the opening performances I remember a fight starting in the audience among those who were in favour of it, and those who were against, and as I stood in the bar afterwards I saw a girl pass by, her evening dress half torn off;

I must say I could not but secretly admire a race who took their art so seriously.

But Joyce only went once or twice. He said it was a passing fashion, and seemed to despise the furore it had created.

The one art besides literature he really cared about was music; for Dubliners have always been crazy about music. They will queue for hours to see a visiting opera company; and what they liked, and still do, are the old fashioned operas by Verdi, Donizetti, Cimarosa, and Rossini, the Italian 'bel canto'.

It was the tenor voice he admired; I never heard him admire a woman's voice, a Gallicurchi or a Melba; in fact when I knew him he was inclined to be cynical about women in general, for once in a moment of innocent enthusiasm, I asked him what Italian women were like – 'Cold,' he replied, 'like all women.'

It was the male voice which attracted, and this accounted for his admiration of Sullivan, the Irish tenor, which became an obsession in the end; he would worry all his influential friends to go and hear Sullivan, and eventually through his persistent efforts succeeded in getting him on to Covent Garden, but only for one or two performances, I think. I never heard this singer, but Budgeon, his friend and biographer, is reported to have said, 'he had a voice like the Forth Bridge'; and Jo Davidson said much the same thing. But Joyce thought he was the greatest of tenors, maintaining obstinately that no voice like his had been heard for fifty years, seeing in him, perhaps, his own frustrated ambition.

Indeed, all the Joyce family sang; his father, himself, and

his son whom he had trained as a singer – so that one could truly say with Joyce that where there was no singing there was no joy. One of my lasting memories of him is how somewhere about midnight he used to cross the room in the same Square Robiac, and sitting down at the piano try his hand on the keyboard letting his fingers run in a musical ripple over the notes when he would sing in his light tenor voice those mocking, ironic, and melancholy Irish songs, a fundamental source of his inspiration, and whose threads he wove and re-wove to form the dark and complicated tapestry of *Finnegans Wake*, songs which like his family portrait he carried with him everywhere he went, and finally turned to for consolation.

Lucia, his daughter, took up dancing. I saw her dance several times, and she promised very well. Once at an international concourse at the Bal Bullier, if she did not get first prize, she was acclaimed by the audience who cried out in enthusiasm, 'L'Irlandaise – L'Irlandaise.' But her father was against it. He thought that she lacked the necessary physical qualifications, and said something about 'women getting up on the stage and waving their arms about', and remarked that 'a girl should learn to walk into a room properly, that is enough'. She gave it up, and at his suggestion took up book illumination. But in secret she was frustrated. The trouble with the children of a famous man is that they are inclined to suffer from a continual inferiority complex. Everyone is interested in the father, and not in them; and though Joyce tried to draw her into the current of life, she resisted secretly and was only willing, as was natural, to accept life on her own terms.

But I remember her as a sensitive and silent girl sitting at the restaurant table, reminding me rather of one of Marie Laurencin's demoiselles, mysterious and evasive, though later I believe she became troublesome and dominant; and as her illness increased, she became to his dismay more hostile to him while he tried to retain her affection in circumstances of increasing difficulty. For Joyce, for whom Creation, Origin, and Paternity were the secret of being, no tragedy could have gone deeper, and the image of his sick child tortured him, for with his peculiar theories of paternity he considered himself as the father, the guilty source. He took her from clinic to clinic, even to Professor Jung in Switzerland, who, as a matter of fact, disliked Joyce and his works, and had jibed that *Ulysses* meant as much read backwards as forwards, and that at any other time in the past it would never have reached the printer; Lucia herself expressed her own resentment of Jung by saying – 'To think that such a big fat materialistic Swissman should try and get hold of my soul.'

But Joyce, as her father, thought that he understood her best. He hoped by some miracle of paternal love that he would bring about her cure, for she acted on him as the ghost had acted on Hamlet.

Around Joyce in Paris were collected a number of progressive writers; Americans for the most part. One was Hemingway, a tall, well-built, handsome fellow, in whose swagger was something of a buccaneer. He was then making his first essays in original prose, an expression of the American mind, differing as it does from the European mind. In Joyce's flat at the periodical reading of his 'work in progress' he used to be there bringing with him a fine fresh air atmosphere, with his big gestures and a resonant laugh.

I remember once he and Padraic Colum, the Irish writer, having a joke about their not having a 'carte d'identité'. Padraic had found a woman's purse, evidently that of a poor woman, in the taxi on his way to Joyce's flat, and was very anxious to return it to the police station.

'But have you got a "carte d'identité"?' he asked.

No, he had not one.

'Then,' I told him, 'I would not go to the police station if I were you. They won't care a rap about the purse, but they will put you in prison for not having a "carte d'identité".'

'That's true,' joined in Hemingway; 'you can do nothing without it. A man can come and hit you in the face, but you dare not hit him back because you have not got a "carte d'identité" – a man can knock you down, he can take your money, your wife, – but if you have no . . .' But further elaboration was cut short by Joyce in his white coat, a short white coat like a dentist's which he always wears when working, sitting down at a table, and wearing very strong spectacles, to read the manuscript of some 'work in progress'. After listening awhile to this strange incantation, which I take it represents the sleep or nocturnal consciousness, as *Ulysses* represents the fantastical day consciousness, of the city, I turned and looked surreptiously at my fellow listeners, and wondered what they were thinking. Hemingway sat looking straight before him, resolute and determined like a Roman soldier, showing little outward evidence of his modernity; Colum, elusive, but sympathetic, his round head, which always had a boyish air, drooped to one side.

Meanwhile, Joyce had quitted his flat in the Square Robiac, and in the course of his endless peregrinations had gone to London to arrange his remarriage. I visited him there and found him living at this time in a dark and uncomfortable flat in Camden Grove in Kensington, a place which he nicknamed 'Camden Grave'. But after a few months he left it to return to Paris to a place in the Avenue St. Philibert. But what with his increasing troubles now added to by the news of his father's death in Dublin, which he took very badly, the stage now began to darken for him so that he composed a new tragic but not unhumorous calendar of the weekdays starting with – 'Moansday, Tearsday, Wailsday, Thumpsday, Frightday, Shatterday'.

Then, the lease of that flat falling in, he took himself, his wife, and Lucia off to Switzerland; he for his eyes, and Lucia for psychiatric treatment. When again they returned to Paris they fixed themselves in the Rue Galilée, off the Champs Elysées. And it was here that I met him for the last time, calling one afternoon.

I had not seen him for several years for I had been living in Waterford, battling with the difficulties of running the family estate, a constant daily round of farming, and also trying to maintain a disintegrating Georgian mansion a thousand miles away from the Parisian world of art and letters, where the names of Modigliani, Pascin, Braque, had never been heard of, and even that of Joyce was but a faint echo.

He invited me that evening to Fouquets, an expensive

restaurant, the most expensive, in fact, on the Champs Elysées, which he now frequented. Sitting at the far end of the table surrounded by the fashionable clientele, detached and observant. I watched Joyce sipping his wine surrounded by the Jolas family who had then taken possession of him.

But I felt a gulf had risen between us as was natural perhaps over so many years, and due to such different experiences, while the atmosphere which surrounded him seemed to me to be very artificial. From what I could overhear of the conversation, it seemed to consist chiefly of quibbling over the possible extension in the meaning of individual words, and suchlike literary hair-splitting. Joyce noticed my attitude and remarked not without justice – 'You look more and more like a farmer' – which was fair enough. I had not liked *Finnegans Wake* and had told him so. Indeed worse I thought, though I had remained silent about it, that he had wasted many vital creative years and would perhaps have done better to have taken Tuohy's sarcastic advice; but then, what do we know of the strange psychological changes an artist may undergo.

Next day, I called to say goodbye. Collapsing as was his habit on a seat in the hall he repeated some of the criticisms that had been levelled against his work, quoting Wyndham Lewis's jibe about him being a middle-class writer, something I did not and could not understand, and which had a Fascist origin anyway; but, there for a moment, I was face to face with the former human and ever-kind Joyce, free from that coterie of hangers-on and publicists for ever busy sunning themselves on his fame; the man of Dublin, Trieste, Pola, and those early days in Paris, still unchanged. I thought how fame, like a marionette, turning in a glitter before the public gaze is only a projection of a personality so to speak, while its projector, the real man of flesh and blood, continues to live his everyday life in spite of, and even contrary to it, escaping nothing. And as I turned to go down the stairs, we both raised our hands on what was to be a final farewell.

Then, in the papers, one read of his hegira in the terror and confusion of war to Switzerland, and to Zürich where he still hoped to find peace and security, remembering his former days there during the 1914 war, while Hitler's demoniac world crashed slowly but inevitably to pieces around him.

For some years he had been suffering from internal pains which his American friends had diagnosed wrongly as of nervous origin, which suited Joyce. It was, however, a duodenal which perforated. An emergency operation was carried out, and he seemed to recover, but, passing into a coma, he died without regaining consciousness.

Some years later I happened to be in Paris when I met Nora, his wife, who had come there on business. I asked her where she would like to go and dine. She said 'The Café Francis'. But it was a mistake, and that evening was a very unhappy one for her with former memories crowding in. As she limped painfully to the waiting taxi, I heard her mutter aloud, 'this too, too solid flesh', for she did not want to continue; this charming, natural woman, always kind and friendly, and who through the troubled sea of married life from the darkness of obscurity to the high-lights of fame had always managed to hold her family together with her courage, and rock-firm common sense. It is true that she was not an intellectual in any sense;

and why should she be? But nevertheless, she was a sincere and gallant woman, and his worthy companion and mate – this breath of Galway air in the intellectual hothouse of Paris.

In April 1951 she died of uremic poisoning brought on by the treatment for her arthritis, and she was buried in the same cemetery as her husband, but, typical of their wandering life, some way apart. I believe that has been rectified, and, re-interred, they lie side by side in the snow-covered Fluntern cemetery outside the lake-reflecting town of Zürich where so much of *Ulysses* was conceived and written.

And so that story ends; so ends the life of this extraordinary man who mirrored back the life of his native city with zest, humour, mimicry, and devilment, and who during his life refused all compromise and concession, who hated any form of narrow-mindedness, and who as an artist never faltered or wrote a commercial line. And when the golden carpet would have been laid out for him wherever he cared to go, he shut himself up into a monumental silence, and set himself to write his new work, still wandering as his Greek hero had wandered, yet always fixed in his purpose, carrying with him as a seafarer might carry some magic talisman to bring him at last safely to his destination – this image of his island home.

Sean Lester

1888–1959

JOHN ERNEST LESTER came from Ulster Protestant stock and was educated at Methodist College, Belfast. He became involved with the nationalist movement as a young man in Belfast through the Gaelic League. When he came to Dublin he became news editor of the *Freeman's Journal*. In 1929, by now in the public service of the new Free State, he was sent to the League of Nations in Geneva where he was the Irish delegate. He was High Commissioner in Danzig when World War Two broke out, and at that point he took over as acting Secretary-General in Geneva.

Lester remained at his post throughout the war years. The Minister for Transport in the British post-war Labour government, Philip Noel-Baker, wrote of him:

I like to think of Sean Lester at that moment in 1940 when he assumed his charge, and when I do, the words of Seneca come into my mind: 'with nothing to hope for he despaired of nothing'. The Assembly and the United Nations have justified his great courage and hope.

Sean Lester had lived beside me in Fairfield Park, Rathgar, Dublin, and as a schoolboy I met him on a few occasions when he was back on leave from Geneva. By chance the next owner of the house was Professor Harry Thrift of Trinity College Dublin, a noted mathematician and international rugby player, who makes an appearance in Joyce's *Ulysses* in a quarter mile flat race which takes place in the college park as the Vice Regal cavalcade passes by outside on Nassau Street.

Thither of the wall the quartermile flat handycappers, M.C. Green, **H. Thrift**, T.M. Patey, C. Scaife, J.B. Jeffs, G.N. Morphy, F. Stevenson, C. Adderly and W.C. Huggard started in pursuit.

His son-in-law Douglas Gageby wrote Sean Lester's biography, from which this extract is taken.

JAMES JOYCE ARRIVED with his family in Geneva on Sunday, 15 December 1940. Lester dates this entry in his diary Monday, 16 December:

I had some correspondence with and about James Joyce and his family. On Sunday morning got a telephone message from the Richemond Hotel, they had arrived there. I spent three hours with them in the afternoon before they caught their train for Lausanne.

The famous Joyce is tall, slight, in the fifties, blue eyes and a good thatch of hair. No one would hesitate in looking at him to recognise his nationality and his accent is as Dublin as when he left it over thirty years ago. His eyesight is very bad and he told me it had been saved some years ago for him by the famous Vogt of Zürich, who had also operated on de Valera. His son, seemingly in the late twenties, came in first. A fine, well-built fellow, with a peculiar hybrid accent in English. He told me he is a singer and has sung in Paris and New York. He is married to an American girl and I had the secret hope that, energetic as he seemed, he was no mere hanger-on.

Joyce and I soon got on intimate terms. He is completely unspoilt by his world success. Natural and pleasant in manner. I told him I had read very early his small book of poems *Chamber Music*; then *Dubliners* and had reviewed the *Portrait of the Artist as a Young Man* (having first assured myself that he had no recollection, I said I had done it for the *Freeman's Journal*); and although I had not re-read the book for fifteen years, I still remembered very vividly the first chapter in which he described a Parnellite household in the crisis of the '90s; I am sure the review was very inadequate. I then told him that I had tried to read *Ulysses* but had to confess I never read it all. I remembered the impression of splashes of beauty, but the Dublin 'argot' at times beat me; I had often wondered how on earth foreigners got along with it. He told me it had been translated into French, German, Czech, Russian, Swedish and, I think, Italian. When I ventured my remark on the incomprehensibility of parts of it, Joyce said that he too had sometimes wondered what the Monsieur in Tokyo made of the Japanese translation. There was a touch of humour in his voice which showed me I had not been trampling too much and in too grave a way on his susceptibilities.

He asked me if I had read *Finnegans Wake*. I said I had read scraps of it when it was being published in *Transition*. He said it was even worse than *Ulysses* and had taken seventeen years to write. I said: 'Is it a big book? I have not seen it yet'; and he replied: 'That reminds me of the story of the drunken Irishman walking from Drogheda to Dundalk and when questioned as to the length of the road, said it was not the length that worried him, it was the width!' He told me he has also published a book with the title something like *Thirteen Poems for a Penny** (reminiscent of D.

---

* This was a small book of Joyce's poems, *Pomes Penyeach*, published in July 1927 by Shakespeare & Company.

Kelleher's commercial display on the Strand). He then began to rake up mutual acquaintances. He had shaken the dust of Dublin off his feet some years before I arrived there. I told him I was an Antrim man who spent his early life in Belfast. 'You need not tell me,' he replied (my accent always sharpens again when I am with Irish people). His father came from Cork, he said: his wife from Galway and he came from Dublin, so we were a representative group. He spoke of Oliver Gogarty about whom he enquired and about his hotel in the West. I had never met John Eglinton. He kept coming back to Herbert Hughes, the Northern musician who spent so much time in London; I had met him not long before his death and liked him very much, but told him of my wife's long acquaintanceship with him. Hughes, he said, had published a peculiar book of at least a dozen of Joyce's poems, having them set to music by twelve composers all of different nationalities. A nice little international tribute to Joyce. I mentioned Desmond FitzGerald's name with a very faint response. Dick Hayes, he knew only by name. As to Lennox Robinson, he inquired whether he was a particular friend of mine. I said I knew him fairly well and then he referred to a series of dramatic competitions given over the Dublin wireless; they ended after a couple of weeks, or rather the adjudication was changed; describing some of the adjudications by Robinson, he said that there was not the slightest doubt the man was completely tight; he had two adjectives which he employed without any other qualification for each of the competitors.

John Dulanty, the High Commissioner in London, he liked and respected very much and he talked of John Sullivan who was born in Cork, but left at the age of three for Paris, and who apparently became a fairly renowned singer in Europe. For Count O'Kelly, he spoke of his ability to write beautiful French, and when I mentioned Gerald's brochure on '*les Petits vins*', disclosed that it was he who introduced Gerald to the Clos de St. Patrice, probably, he thought, the oldest vineyard in France; the Château-Neuf du Pape was comparatively young and, in his view, seemed to be more or less a descendant of the St. Patrice. I ventured a remark that it was not a wine worthy of the great name and he said, laughingly, that he would never drink it himself. There was another St. Patrice on the Loire where the tradition was that St. Patrick on his Rome pilgrimage had crossed the river on his mantle and on arriving at the other side had planted his blackthorn stick. The parish priest in the village had told him that this had grown and flowered always in December and the shrub or tree was known as the '*fleur de St. Patrice*'. Unfortunately, during the last war the Sacristan, or gardener, had a '*crise de nerfs*' following family losses and had hacked down the ancient bush.

Joyce told me that he had only spent ten days in Ireland during the last thirty years – some day I hope I shall get the story of his departure from him. He seemed to have gone first to Trieste, where he taught English. His children were born there and they did not speak any English until they were twenty, and in the family asides over the tea-table, I noticed it was always in Italian. I said to Joyce, 'Why do you not go home? I myself would like so much to do so.'

'I am attached to it daily and nightly like an umbilical cord': the family, who had gathered by this time, joined in protest, as it was true he kept Radio Eireann going on the wireless all the time. His son intervened and said 'One thing I am thankful to be in Switzerland for, is that I can now have a room of my own'; they had been living for six months in a tiny village, forty kilometres from Vichy. Joyce then began to discuss with him all sorts of details of the daily programme; the son was outraged by the quality of opera broadcast. I said: 'I enjoyed the folklore songs most of all.' We laughed together over the last *Question Time*, when the three girl-typists gave some screamingly funny replies. The only one I could remember was when one of them was asked the precise meaning of a 'bourgeois' and replied 'an Italian soldier'. Then Joyce remarked that one of the competitors, the one who got top-marks on the previous Sunday, when asked who had won such and such a literary prize two years ago, had replied, 'I am not sure, but I think it was Joyce'; there were short controversies with the competitor, but he was adjudicated correct. Joyce said that when the Dublin labourer gave this reply, which was correct, he stood up and bowed to the wireless.

They were going to settle in Zürich, where they had some good friends. I said I thought it was an unusual place for him to choose and asked, what about Suisse Romande? His wife then intervened and said that Zürich had always been associated with certain crises in their life: they had rushed from Austria at the beginning of the last war and had lived in Zürich very comfortably; they had spent their honeymoon there; it was there that Joyce's eyesight had been saved and now they were going back in another crisis. They like the stolid virtues of the people. Joyce, describing any Saturday night dinner in a restaurant when a score of men, fat and square-headed, would sit eating a great meal talking the patois of which he could not understand a word, while the wives stayed at home darning socks and cleaning silver until they were allowed out on the Sunday night. Joyce said he often wondered whether he had not been expelled from France because of his strongly expressed conviction that Switzerland's white wine (he only drinks white wine) was vastly superior to anything he drank in France.

They had left their place in Paris in May; it was filled with most precious books, first editions and presentations from all over the world, and with many good pictures. He had, he told me, some Jack Yeats' and asked about Paul Henry, whom we also admired.

Gossiping afterwards, he told me that he had been a rival to the young McCormack and in their early days in Dublin, his wife had sometimes tried to persuade him to follow the musical career and drop the writing. This was at a time when he was having a hard struggle and apparently it was 'a near thing'. Mrs Joyce – showing more signs of her cosmopolitan life, pleasant voice – joined in deploring McCormack's pathetic and tragic insistence on continuing to sing as he did when his voice had gone.

Joyce's practical blindness was most noticeable over the tea; he asked his wife to prepare a piece of toast for him and then decided with slight pathos to have biscuits, which were easy to find. Shaking hands with him, I noticed his wife, who acted as his eyes, indicated to him to hold out his hand. When I asked him if he had read one or two recent books, mentioned Desmond Ryan's book of recollections, he showed me his difficulties; he has two glasses, one, a small magnifying glass which he has to use for reading, and when he writes he has another glass which must be affixed to his spectacles, and each time he had to read something while writing he has to make a change; obviously the poor fellow can read very little and slowly: one can understand the radio!

The second time I mentioned the question of his returning home, his wife said she had been trying to induce him to for the last two or three years. Joyce said nothing, but when I spoke of getting home in the present circumstances, he said the journey would have been quite possible for him, but he felt it would not be very dignified to go home in the present circumstances. Speaking about the daughter who has had a bad nervous breakdown and has been in a sanatorium for two or three years, he said she was a very gentle and sweet creature; he apparently had gone to visit her every weekend and that at first Sean Murphy [the Irish minister to Paris] obtained permission from the Germans to leave the occupied zone; O'Kelly, who had acted for Murphy, said that when the application was made to the German Commandant in Paris, the latter granted it at once, having read and admired Joyce's work. The visa given by their Vichy government for the exit of his son, in view of very strict application of the rule preventing foreigners, and especially belligerents (the Joyces all had British passports) under the age of forty to leave the country, was difficult to understand and had astonished them. The application had been made for the four visas: Joyce, wife, son and eight-year-old grandson; they did not understand how it had been granted, but perhaps it was again the magic of Joyce's name.

Less than a month later Joyce was dead. Lester wrote to Mrs. Joyce on 13 January:

Dear Mrs. Joyce,
I have just received a telephone message from Zürich, telling me of your husband's death. It has been a great

shock to me and I want to send at once a message of my deep sympathy. I had just signed the enclosed letter to him.

It was for me a delightful experience to have met him during your hurried passage through Geneva. I found him so charming and so unspoiled by his world fame and I was looking forward with very real pleasure to spending some good evenings with him. I am not going to say anything about the loss to literature in the poignancy of your own bereavement, but, believe me, I sympathise with all my heart and share in the sense of loss which all his friends must feel.
Yours very sincerely,
Seán Lester

P.S. I wish to attend the funeral and if I can possibly leave my post for the time, I shall be there; my responsibilities here are unhappily very heavy and may prevent my leaving.

Lester did not go to Zürich for the funeral. He suggested to Frank Cremins, chargé at Zürich, that he might like to go so that some official Irish person would be there. 'F. won't, says he can't leave. Too busy coding and decoding telegrams.'

Lester received a first reply to his letter, dated 18 January 1941:

Dear Mr. Lester,
Thank you very much for your letter of January 14th. We were sad not to have you, a compatriot of

Mr. Joyce at the funeral. Lord Derwent spoke very
well, also Professor Hanman. We had a tenor sing
Monteverdi and Handel. It was a white and cold day
and the sun was pale. I had the death mask made
even more; a facsimile made of Mr. Joyce's head with
his wonderful ear also on it. If the Irish State is interested in it perhaps they could write. At any rate I am
going to have a copy made for Zürich and for
myself.

I should very much like to meet you some time as
you were always so kind to help Mr. Joyce.

Yours very sincerely,

Dr Carola Giedion-Welcker

And another, from George Joyce in Zürich, dated 8
February:

Dear Mr. Lester,

Many thanks for your kind letter to my mother, please
excuse her for not answering it herself but she is yet
much too upset to be able to attend to any correspondence. Many thanks also for the beautiful wreath
you sent to my father's funeral.

I know my father was very pleased to have had the
pleasure of meeting you during our short stay in
Geneva. He was looking forward to meeting you soon
again and having a real home evening in your company. Unfortunately fate decided otherwise.

As far as my sister's affairs are concerned I really
don't know what I should do. Naturally I would like

to carry out my father's wishes and have her brought here to Switzerland. I suppose the best way will be to get her an Irish passport. On the other hand I imagine this is going to be a very costly affair. So I shall have to wait until I know exactly what our financial situation is going to be.

My mother begs me to thank you for all you have tried to do for my sister and wishes to be kindly remembered to you.

Sincerely yours,

George Joyce

Lester writes in his diary for 4 February 1941:

The Times notice on Joyce quotes what it describes as 'the extremes of opinion' on his work. Sir Edmund Gosse wrote 'the worthlessness and impudence of his writings'; while the middle, puzzled state of mind is typified by AE's remark, 'I don't know whether you are a fountain or a cistern.' (I think the nice mind has changed the word cesspool for cistern.) 'In his student days' – says *The Times* – 'he was so self-opinionated and vain that he said to W.B. Yeats: 'We have met too late; you are too old to be influenced by me', to which the poet made answer, 'Never have I encountered so much pretension with so little to show for it.'

They also record (a thing that I had forgotten) that Joyce went back to Dublin to start the Volta Cinema in 1912. I am pleased to see in conclusion of this notice: 'In person Joyce was gentle and kindly, living a laborious life in his Paris flat tended by his devoted, humorous wife.'

Elsie [Lester's wife, who was living in Dublin] tells me that the Irish newspapers have been very unsympathetic, referring to him as an author who was born in Ireland. One would expect the orthodox to wash their hands of one who challenged orthodoxy so impudently. She adds that a few 'poseurs' like Con Curran and Kenneth Reddin published some notes of their recollections; I agree they were probably intended as self-advertising.